# The Execution Reliability Advantage

# The Execution Reliability Advantage

How Leaders Turn Improvement Activity into Sustained Operating Results

Darren Dolcemascolo

Published by EMS Consulting Group, Inc.

# Copyright



Published by EMS Consulting Group, Inc.

Carlsbad, California

www.emsstrategies.com

First edition.

ISBN: 979-8-9964427-0-6

The examples in this book are based on the author's experience working with organizations in manufacturing, healthcare, biotech, service, and related industries. Some details have been modified, combined, or generalized to protect confidentiality. The principles, lessons, and operating patterns remain representative of real improvement and execution challenges.

This book is intended for general business and educational purposes. It does not provide legal, financial, regulatory, or accounting advice. Readers should apply the concepts in light of their own business conditions, professional judgment, and organizational requirements.

# Dedication

To my family:

To my wife, Cari, for 27 years of love, support, patience, and partnership.

To my parents, whose guidance and example helped shape the person I became.

And to my creative and talented daughter, Alyssa, with love and gratitude.

# Praise for The Execution Reliability Advantage

"The challenge facing many organizations is not a lack of improvement initiatives, but the inability to consistently translate those initiatives into sustained business results. Darren's Execution Reliability framework provides leaders with a practical and disciplined approach for closing the gap between activity and performance, emphasizing leadership ownership, operating cadence, capability building, and follow-through.

I have long appreciated Darren's thoughtful approach, having first worked with Darren and EMS Consulting Group in 2008. Darren is not only a Lean Six Sigma expert, but a consummate professional who takes the time needed to teach and develop his clients - truly teaching the client to fish rather than simply providing the answer. This differentiates Darren from his peers, and I have witnessed this commitment firsthand on several occasions.

Darren helps organizations build the capabilities and execution discipline necessary to sustain improvements over time. This book caused me to reflect on the valuable insights and contributions Darren has made over the years. In *The Execution Reliability Advantage*, he offers executives and operational leaders a practical pathway for turning strategy into action, delivering measurable results, and sustaining competitive advantage."

**Dave Mowry**
Chief Executive Officer
Breg, Inc.

"Darren describes a problem that I know very well from my own experience: improvement work that begins with energy but does not reach the business result. At RE:CIRCLE, the improvements that lasted — including our pre-consumer food waste diversion work — lasted because of exactly what this book asks for: leadership ownership, a regular operating cadence, and follow-through that confirms what has really changed in the work. I recommend this book to every executive who is no longer satisfied with improvement activity that does not translate into sustained performance."

**Clemens J. Stockreiter**
Founder
RE:CIRCLE Solutions

"During the early stages of Blue-White Industries' Lean journey, Darren Dolcemascolo and EMS Consulting Group provided us with a valuable foundation in operational improvement. We experienced firsthand how much improvement activity can exist without producing sustained execution reliability and business results.

*The Execution Reliability Advantage* offers leaders practical guidance on establishing clear business focus, leadership ownership, operating cadence, and rigorous follow-through to turn improvement efforts into lasting performance. This message aligns closely with our work building Be-WISE as our company's operating system.

I recommend this book to any executive or operations leader responsible for converting continuous improvement into measurable, sustainable success."

**Rob Gledhill**
President & CEO
Blue-White Industries, Ltd.

"*The Execution Reliability Advantage* addresses one of the most common gaps in operational improvement: the difference between improvement activity and sustained business performance. Darren's focus on starting with the business condition, then connecting the work to ownership, cadence, problem solving, and follow-through, is practical and highly relevant for executives and operations leaders. This book gives leaders a clear operating lens for turning good improvement work into measurable and sustainable results."

**Sorin Gorgan**
Sr. VP, Manufacturing Operations
Broadata Communications, Inc.

"Whether you are new to Lean or have years of experience leading improvement efforts, this book addresses a challenge many organizations face: turning good ideas into lasting results. Darren provides a practical framework for understanding why improvement efforts stall and what leaders can do to sustain change and drive measurable business performance. This is a valuable resource for anyone responsible for improving operations and delivering results."

**Jesse Rendon**
VP of Operations
CEMCO

"I had the privilege of working directly with Darren Dolcemascolo of EMS Consulting Group as we implemented Lean operations strategies at Flux Power. Under his guidance, we increased productivity by 40% and significantly reduced waste across our operation — results that came not from theory, but from disciplined, repeatable execution on the floor.

That same practical rigor comes through on every page of *The Execution Reliability Advantage.* Darren has a rare ability to turn Lean principles into concrete actions that teams can actually sustain, and this book distills the methods that delivered real, measurable improvement in our business. Any leader serious about building an operation that performs reliably — day in and day out — will find it indispensable."

**Jeff Mason**
COO
Flux Power

"*The Execution Reliability Advantage* is an essential read for leaders and professionals striving to bridge the gap between improvement activity and sustained business performance. It emphasizes the critical importance of identifying the underlying business condition before selecting tools or solutions, ensuring that improvement efforts are targeted and impactful. By advocating for cross-functional input and disciplined problem-solving, the book helps prevent short-term fixes and fosters long-term, reliable execution. Leaders responsible for operational performance will find its practical guidance invaluable in creating meaningful and lasting improvements."

**Kelly Kemp**
Sr. Director, Process Development Engineering
Vertex Pharmaceuticals

# Acknowledgments

This book reflects many years of working with leaders, teams, colleagues, clients, and friends who were willing to engage in the practical work of improving real operating performance. I am grateful to the many people who trusted me with their challenges, shared their experience, and helped shape the way I think about improvement, leadership, and execution.

I want to especially acknowledge the late Dave Godfrey, who taught me much about the consulting business early in my career. His guidance helped me understand not only the importance of technical knowledge, but also the importance of judgment, trust, and serving clients well. I am also grateful to Pete Glaser for his mentoring advice and friendship, and to Ken Flaherty for his friendship, perspective, and thoughtful feedback over the years.

I have also been fortunate to work with many leaders and clients who helped me learn from real business conditions, not just from theory. I am especially grateful to Kermit Stott, Frank Karg, Dave Mowry, Jorgine Ellerbrock, Joan Haab, Jesse Rendon, Sorin Gorgan, Kelly Kemp, and Rob Gledhill, along with the many other leaders and improvement professionals who have contributed to my learning through their trust, candor, and commitment to better performance.

Thank you also to those who reviewed early material, provided feedback, offered endorsements, and encouraged the development of this book. Their comments reinforced the need for a practical executive discussion about turning improvement activity into sustained operating results.

Finally, I am deeply grateful to my family for their support, patience, and encouragement. Their presence and support have made this work possible.

My hope is that the ideas here serve leaders and teams who are trying to make improvement work matter in the real operating conditions of their organizations.

# Author's Note

This book is based on many years of working with organizations that were trying to improve real operating conditions: lead time, delivery, quality, productivity, inventory, project execution, capability development, daily management, and leadership follow-through.

The examples are intentionally generalized. In some cases, details have been changed, combined, or simplified to protect client confidentiality and to make the operating lesson clearer. The purpose is not to tell the story of one company. The purpose is to show the patterns that often determine whether improvement activity becomes sustained operating performance.

Throughout the book, I use Lean, Six Sigma, value stream mapping, problem solving, training, coaching, advisory support, and AI-enabled support as examples. These methods can be very useful. However, the central argument is broader: improvement work produces better results when leaders connect it to the business condition, objectives, measures, value, system view, problem-solving discipline, capability building, leadership ownership, operating cadence, and follow-through.

That is the execution reliability advantage.

# Table of Contents

# Introduction: Why Good Improvement Work Still Fails

Many organizations invest heavily in improvement and still struggle to turn that effort into sustained results.

They may have the right methods, capable people, and good intentions. They may hold workshops, launch projects, train employees, create dashboards, and assign action items. However, if the work is not connected to the business condition, leadership ownership, operating cadence, and follow-through, the improvement effort may not produce sustained results.

That is the execution reliability problem.

Execution reliability is the organization's ability to translate intent into action, action into measurable progress, and progress into sustained performance.

This book is about the operating conditions that make that possible.

## How I Came to This Work

My interest in operations and improvement began before I had the language for Lean, Six Sigma, or execution reliability.

Just before I entered Columbia University as a freshman, I attended an event where each engineering department presented what its discipline did. When I reached Industrial Engineering and Operations Research, the message was simple and practical: the field was about getting the biggest bang for the buck, or creating the most value from the resources available.

That idea immediately appealed to me. It described practical work: improving systems, making better decisions, using resources wisely, and creating measurable value.

After doing operations improvement and management work for several years in multiple industries, I started EMS Consulting Group in 2003. From the beginning, our focus was on helping leadership teams improve operating performance in practical, measurable ways. We performed assessments, trained at all levels, facilitated improvement workshops, and provided coaching.

## The Pattern That Repeats

In the early years of my work, the focus was often on teaching tools and facilitating improvement activities. That work was valuable, and it still is.

Organizations needed help understanding flow, waste, variation, root causes, standard work, and project execution.

But after working with many organizations, a broader pattern became clear.

The organizations that sustained improvement did more than use tools. They connected improvement to business priorities. Leaders were involved. Problems were made visible. Work was reviewed through a cadence. Participants received coaching. Action plans were followed up. Standards were reinforced. The management system changed enough to support the new way of working.

The organizations that struggled often had many of the same tools, but the tools were not embedded in the DNA of the organization.

The difference was not simply technical knowledge.

The difference was the operating system around the improvement work.

By operating system, I do not mean software. I mean the way the organization manages the business: how priorities are selected, how work is reviewed, how problems are surfaced, how decisions are made, how resources are allocated, how people are coached, how standards are reinforced, and how follow-up occurs.

When the operating system supports improvement, the tools have a much better chance of producing value. When the operating system does not support improvement, even good tools can produce only limited results.

## Why Improvement Activity Is Not Enough

Most organizations do not suffer from a lack of activity.

A company may have an active continuous improvement program and still struggle with late deliveries, high inventory, poor quality, slow decisions, weak project execution, or recurring problems. Another organization may have trained many people but still have limited application. Another may have daily huddles but still rely on expediting and heroic effort to meet commitments.

Leaders must distinguish between improvement activity and execution reliability.

Improvement activity includes the events, tools, meetings, projects, training, and documentation associated with improvement. Execution reliability is the organization's ability to consistently translate intent into action, action into measurable progress, and progress into sustained performance.

Improvement activity can support execution reliability, but only when it is connected to the right business condition and supported by leadership ownership, cadence, problem solving, capability development, and follow-through.

This issue matters now because many leaders are facing operating pressure from several directions at once. Delivery expectations are higher. Inventory and cash discipline matter more. Margin pressure leaves less room for waste, rework, and delay. ERP and technology initiatives require clearer business processes and stronger follow-through. Teams are busy, but leaders still need better execution across functions, decisions, projects, and daily work.

## The Execution Reliability Model

Execution reliability can be understood as a practical operating model. It is not a separate program or methodology. It is a way to think about the conditions that must be in place for improvement work to become sustained business performance.

The model includes eight connected elements:

1. Business Condition — What needs to improve?
2. Objectives, Measures, and Value — What will be different, how will we know, and why does it matter?
3. System View — What flow of work, decisions, handoffs, and constraints produces the current result?
4. Problem-Solving Discipline — How will the organization define problems, understand causes, and test and implement countermeasures?
5. Capability Building — What must people learn, practice, and apply in the work?
6. Leadership Ownership — Who owns the operating system and the result?
7. Operating Cadence — How will performance, problems, escalation, and support be reviewed?
8. Follow-Through and Sustainment — How will action become completed, verified, standardized, and sustained?

Read the model from left to right as a diagnostic sequence. It begins with the business condition, moves through the disciplines required to understand and improve the system, and ends with the routines needed to sustain performance. The sequence is not rigid, but it shows the logic leaders should test before launching more activity.

# Figure 1. The Execution Reliability Model

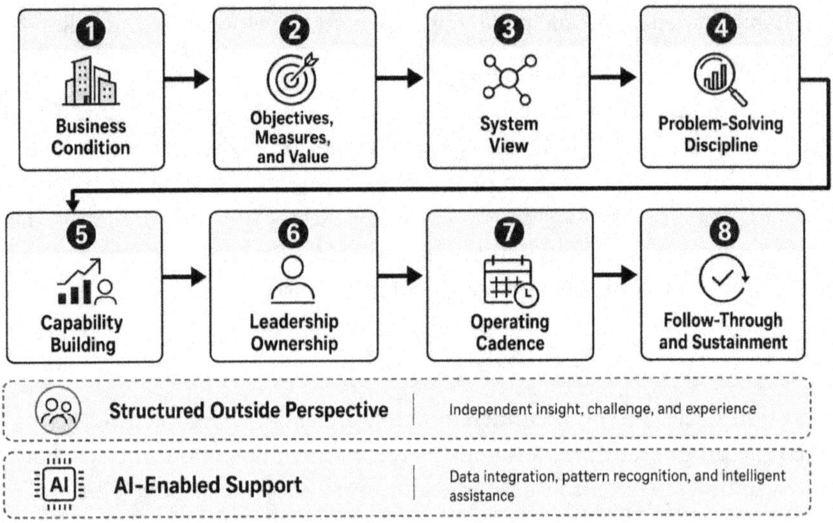


*Support layers strengthen execution reliability. They do not replace leadership ownership.*

### Leadership Application

*Use Figure 1 to locate the weakest part of the execution system. A business condition without measures is difficult to manage. Cadence without follow-through becomes reporting activity. Follow-through without standard work may not hold the gain.*

## What Execution Reliability Means

Execution reliability means that important work moves from decision to action, from action to learning, and from learning to a better way of working. It does not mean perfection. It means the organization can see problems early, respond appropriately, and follow through.

In practical terms, execution reliability depends on the organization's ability to connect the business condition to the way work is managed. Leaders need enough clarity to know what must improve, enough discipline to understand the system and solve problems, enough capability to apply the methods, and enough cadence and follow-through to sustain the gain.

Technology, outside perspective, and improvement methods can support that work. They do not replace leadership ownership of the operating system.

## This Is Not a Tool Book

This book is not a Lean tools manual. It is not a Six Sigma textbook. It is not a book about implementing a specific methodology in a prescribed sequence.

There are many excellent resources that explain improvement tools and methods in detail. I have written, taught, and used many of these methods for years.

However, this book has a different purpose.

The purpose is to help leaders understand why good improvement work often fails to become sustained operating performance and what conditions must be created for improvement to produce results.

The book uses improvement methods as examples, but the main focus is leadership and execution. The methods are discussed because they are useful. They are not the destination.

The destination is better business performance. That may mean shorter lead times, better delivery, lower inventory, higher productivity, better quality, improved cash flow, stronger project execution, more reliable daily management, or less management firefighting. The specific outcome depends on the business condition.

The principle is simple: the method should serve the condition.

## Who This Book Is For

This book is written for leaders who are responsible for improving operating performance.

That includes executives, general managers, operations leaders, functional leaders, continuous improvement sponsors, HR and learning leaders, project sponsors, and internal CI professionals who want improvement work to produce measurable value.

It is also written for leaders who may be frustrated by the gap between effort and results. You may recognize some of these situations:

- Your organization has improvement activity, but results are inconsistent.
- You have trained people, but application is limited.
- You have projects, but follow-through is uneven.
- You have dashboards, but problems still surface late.
- You have daily meetings, but decisions and escalation are weak.

- You have capable people, but priorities keep shifting.
- You have process maps or action plans, but implementation is slow.
- You have a CI function, but improvement is still treated as something outside the way the business is managed.

If any of these situations are familiar, the problem may not be the lack of a method. The problem may be the operating system surrounding the method.

## How the Book Is Organized

The chapters follow the model in a practical sequence. Chapters 1 and 2 clarify the business condition and the agreement required before action. Chapters 3 and 4 focus on seeing the system and solving problems with discipline. Chapters 5 and 6 address capability and leadership ownership. Chapters 7 and 8 turn ownership into cadence and follow-through. Chapters 9 and 10 then explain how outside perspective and AI-enabled support can strengthen, but not replace, the operating system. The conclusion brings the reader back to one starting point: the condition the business needs to improve.

## A Practical Point of View

This book is written from a practical point of view. The ideas come from organizations trying to improve real operating conditions: flow, quality, delivery, project execution, capability transfer, daily management, and leadership follow-through. The details vary, but the pattern is consistent: improvement produces better results when leaders connect the work to business conditions, measures, value, ownership, cadence, and follow-through.

That work begins by asking a simple question:

*What condition of the business must improve, and what system will make that improvement reliable?*

# Chapter 1: Start with the Business Condition, Not the Tool

Improvement conversations often begin with a requested tool or method.

A leader may ask for value stream mapping, 5S, Green Belt training, kaizen support, A3 coaching, daily management, or help before an ERP implementation.

In many cases, the request is reasonable. The tool may be appropriate. The person asking may have a legitimate concern and may be trying to move the organization in the right direction.

The better leadership question is: "What business condition is the organization trying to improve?"

That distinction is important. Business conditions give improvement work its purpose.

By business condition, I mean the current operating situation that leaders need to change. Lead time may be too long. Delivery performance may be inconsistent. Inventory may be tying up cash. Quality problems may be recurring. Capacity may be constrained. Productivity may be below the level needed to support growth. Customer responsiveness may be poor. New product introductions may be delayed. An ERP implementation may be struggling because business processes and decision rights are unclear.

Business conditions define the reason improvement work exists. Leaders should select the method because it fits the condition, not because it is familiar, fashionable, or available.

Many improvement efforts lose focus because the organization starts with the method instead of the condition. People become busy with the workshop, the training, the map, the board, or the project. The activity may be well intended and technically sound, but the connection to business performance is weak.

A tool-first approach often creates activity before the organization has clarified the business condition. A condition-first approach begins with the operating gap, the value at stake, and the result that must improve. Once that condition is clear, leaders can select the method that best fits the problem rather than forcing the problem to fit the tool. This is why the starting question matters.

**Figure 2. Tool-First vs. Condition-First**

*The starting point shapes the quality of execution.*

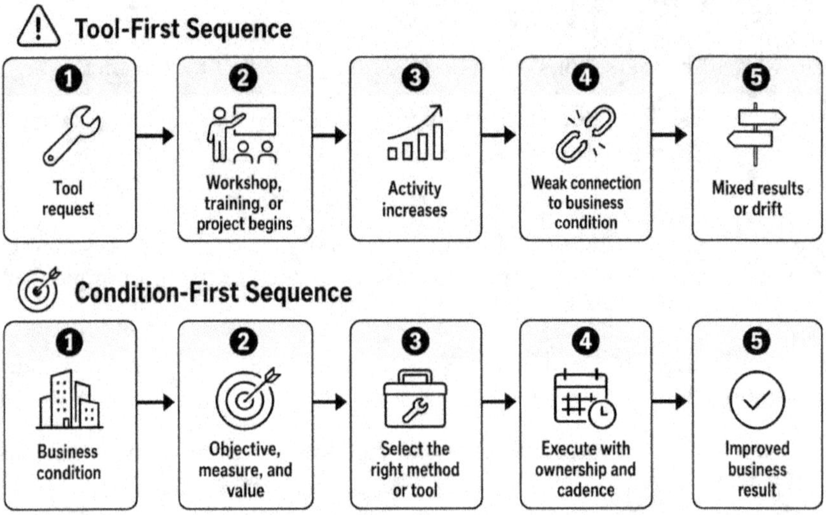


### Leadership Application

*Use Figure 2 as a leadership pause before approving a workshop, training program, kaizen event, or technology effort. If the Tool-First sequence describes the current conversation, the team is probably moving too quickly. Shift the discussion to the flow at the bottom: condition, value, method, ownership, cadence, and follow-through.*

## Where This Chapter Fits in the Execution Reliability Model

This chapter introduces the first element of the Execution Reliability Model: the business condition. Before leaders select a tool, schedule training, launch a project, or ask for outside support, they need to understand what condition of the business must improve.

This matters because execution reliability begins with relevance. A tool can be technically sound and still fail to improve performance if it is not connected to a real operating gap, a measure of success, and a clear reason for action.

The chapters that follow build on this point. Chapter 2 will focus on agreement before action, but that agreement is only useful when it is anchored in the business condition that matters.

## Why Tool Requests Can Be Misleading

Tool requests usually come from a real concern: late orders, excess inventory, poor communication, rework, customer complaints, high overtime, project delays, or poor visibility. The leader then looks for a method that appears to address the concern.

This is understandable. Leaders want action. They may have seen a method work elsewhere, used it at a previous company, or heard that another organization improved performance with a similar approach.

The danger is not that the tool is wrong. The danger is that the tool request may be only a surface description of a deeper problem.

Common examples include:

- A value stream mapping request may actually reflect unstable scheduling, unclear order priorities, poor material availability, slow engineering decisions, or weak cross-functional ownership.
- A 5S request may actually reflect poor process design, lack of standard work, unclear replenishment, weak supervision, or workarounds caused by unreliable material flow.
- A Green Belt training request may actually reflect weak project selection, missing sponsorship, limited coaching, or poor follow-up cadence.

The tool may be part of the answer. It is not always the starting point.

## In Practice: When a Training Request Was Really a Sponsorship Problem

**Situation**

An organization asked for Green Belt training because leaders wanted employees to become better problem solvers. The request was reasonable. Green Belt training could build useful capability, provide a common method, and give participants a structured way to improve quality, cost, delivery, productivity, or customer responsiveness.

**Typical Response**

The typical response was to schedule the course, select participants, deliver the material, and expect improvement projects to follow. The training was well received, and participants learned useful concepts, tools, and language.

However, training alone did not mean the organization had created the conditions for application.

**What Was Actually Happening**

The organization had not selected projects. Sponsors did not know what business objectives the projects should support. Managers supported the idea of training, but they had not committed time for participants to work on projects. The review cadence was unclear. There was no agreement on how progress would be measured, how coaching would be provided, or how leaders would reinforce the use of the methods after the course.

In that situation, the request was training, but the deeper issue was weak sponsorship, weak project selection, and weak follow-through.

**What Changed**

Before approving the training as a stand-alone event, leaders clarified several questions:

- What capability did the organization need to build?
- What business problems should participants work on?
- Who would sponsor the projects?
- How would project progress be reviewed?
- What coaching would participants receive?
- What measures would show whether the training created value?
- How would leaders reinforce the use of the methods after the course?

Once those questions were answered, the same Green Belt content was designed around application. Participants were selected based on role and influence. Projects were scoped before the first session. Sponsors were assigned. Coaching was built into the program. Progress was reviewed on a defined cadence.

**Result**

The training became more than a course. It became part of a capability-transfer system. The work was connected to business conditions, participants had real problems to solve, and leaders had a clearer role in sponsorship, review, and follow-through.

**Execution Reliability Lesson**
Training is useful when it builds capability that can be applied to real work. But the course should serve the business condition, not the other way around.

When leaders ask for training, the better first question is not only, "What course should we run?" It is, "What business condition do we need people to improve, and what sponsorship, coaching, and cadence will help them apply what they learn?"

## Client Example: When Inventory Was the Symptom, Not the Problem

**Situation**
A scaling biotech operation was experiencing rapid inventory growth. Space was becoming constrained, quality exposure was increasing, and leadership believed the organization was beginning to lose control as volume increased.

At first glance, the issue appeared straightforward: too much inventory, not enough space, and a need for Lean tools or inventory reduction efforts.

**Typical Response**
In similar situations, organizations often run inventory reduction events, implement 5S or warehouse reorganization, add temporary storage space, or push teams to reduce inventory levels.

These actions can create activity, and some of them may be useful in the short term. However, they rarely address why inventory is growing in the first place.

**What Was Actually Happening**
When the condition was examined more carefully, inventory was not the core problem. It was the result of system instability.

Flow across processes was inconsistent. Material was being built ahead to compensate for uncertainty. Decisions about release, prioritization, and movement were not governed by a clear cadence. Cross-functional ownership of inventory and flow was weak.

In other words, inventory was accumulating because the operating system could not reliably control flow.

**What Changed**
Instead of starting with an inventory tool, leadership clarified several things:

- The business condition: inventory growth creating risk in space, quality, cash, and scalability
- The value at stake: capacity, control, and scalable growth

- The system view: how material actually flowed across functions
- The ownership model: who was responsible for end-to-end inventory behavior
- The cadence: how flow, constraints, and decisions would be reviewed

The focus shifted from simply reducing inventory to stabilizing the system that produced it.

**Result**
The organization reduced inventory exposure by approximately 50 percent, improved process control, reduced quality risk, and freed operational capacity.

Importantly, the result was not achieved through a one-time reduction effort. It was achieved by improving how the system managed flow.

**Execution Reliability Lesson**
Inventory is rarely the real problem. It is usually the result of how the system is operating.

Organizations that treat inventory only as a target may create temporary reduction. Organizations that improve execution reliability reduce inventory as an outcome of better flow, clearer ownership, and stronger operating cadence.

## The Better First Question

The better first question is simple: what business problem are we trying to solve?

This question should be asked before scheduling training, designing a workshop, selecting the methodology, or launching an initiative. It moves the conversation from activity to outcome.

Several supporting questions are useful:

1. What is happening now that should not be happening?
2. What should be happening that is not happening?
3. How do we know this is a problem?
4. What is the current condition?
5. What is the target condition?
6. What business result would improve if this problem were addressed?
7. How would we measure progress?
8. What value is at stake?

These questions are not complicated, but they change the conversation. Instead of assuming that a requested tool is the answer, the organization begins to clarify the outcome it wants.

This also helps avoid a common operating problem: providing the requested activity while failing to address the condition that actually needs to change.

An internal CI leader, functional leader, or improvement professional creates more value by helping the organization think clearly than by simply accepting the first stated request. This does not mean dismissing the tool. It means understanding why the tool is being requested and whether it is likely to improve the business condition.

In many cases, leaders appreciate this discipline. They do not usually want the tool for its own sake. They want the result they believe the tool will create.

## Tools Are Useful When They Are Properly Connected

This book is not arguing against tools. Tools, methods, training, and structure all matter.

The question is whether the method is connected to the business condition. When it is connected, it helps the organization see something, decide something, improve something, or sustain something that matters.

When it is disconnected, it becomes activity. It may still look professional. It may create documents, charts, boards, reports, and meetings. But it may not change the way the business performs.

This is why the sequence matters.

The stronger sequence is:

1. Understand the business condition.
2. Clarify the objective.
3. Define how success will be measured.
4. Understand the value of improvement.
5. Identify the operating system gap.
6. Select the appropriate method or tool.
7. Establish leadership ownership and cadence.
8. Implement, review, and sustain.

The weaker sequence is:

1. Select the tool.
2. Run the event or training.
3. Create outputs.

4. Hope the business condition improves.

The first sequence creates focus. The second creates motion.

## Do Not Confuse Language with Discipline

One thing I have learned over the years is that organizations should not become too religious about the terminology.

Some organizations use Lean language. Some use Six Sigma language. Some talk about operational excellence, continuous improvement, business process improvement, execution, or performance improvement. Some organizations are comfortable with Japanese terms such as kaizen, gemba, and muda. Others prefer plain English.

The terminology matters less than the discipline.

The real question is not whether people are using the preferred vocabulary. The real question is whether the organization has a disciplined way to define problems, understand current conditions, measure progress, identify causes, test countermeasures, and sustain results.

This does not mean language is unimportant. A shared language can help. It is useful when leaders, managers, and teams have a common way to talk about problems, measures, flow, root causes, countermeasures, and follow-through. But the purpose of that language is to improve thinking and action. It should not become an end in itself.

An organization can use Lean terminology and still fail to improve. Another organization can use very simple language and make meaningful progress because the thinking is sound, the leadership ownership is clear, and the follow-through is strong.

## A Value Stream Mapping Example

A company asks for a value stream mapping workshop because leaders want to improve flow and reduce delays. On the surface, this is a reasonable request. Value stream mapping can help people see how material, information, handoffs, waiting, batching, rework, and decisions affect performance. However, before agreeing that mapping is the right intervention, leaders should clarify the business condition.

- Which value stream is creating the most concern?
- What is the current lead time?
- What is the required lead time?

- Where are customers being affected?
- Which functions are involved?
- Who owns the value stream?
- What decisions will leaders be willing to make after the map is created?

Those questions may confirm that value stream mapping is appropriate. They may also reveal that the organization already understands much of the process, but lacks ownership, decision rights, resources, or cadence for follow-through.

The map can help, but only if the organization is prepared to act on what the map reveals. Otherwise, the workshop may produce a useful current-state map, a reasonable future-state map, and a list of opportunities, but little change in the business condition.

## In Practice: When ERP Readiness Was Really Business-Side Clarity

**Situation**
A company was struggling with an ERP implementation. Leaders wanted better visibility, clearer workflows, fewer handoff problems, and more confidence in the implementation path.

The request appeared reasonable. The organization asked for value stream mapping or process improvement support because leaders believed the current processes needed to be better understood before the system could be configured effectively.

**Typical Response**
The typical response was to treat the issue as a technology or process-documentation problem. The organization scheduled more meetings, asked for more process maps, clarified more requirements, and expected the implementation team to keep moving.

The software team continued to build against the information it had. Business users continued to explain exceptions and workarounds. Leaders continued to ask why progress was slow.

Activity increased, but clarity did not.

**What Was Actually Happening**
The ERP implementation was struggling because the business had not defined the operating model the system was supposed to support.

- Process ownership was unclear.
- Decision rights were not defined.

- Cross-functional requirements were incomplete.
- Future-state workflows had not been agreed upon.
- Data governance was weak.
- Scope control was difficult.
- Success measures were not clear enough.

When those elements were missing, the implementation team was forced to compensate. Developers built against partial knowledge. Requirements changed repeatedly. Users relied on workarounds. Leaders lost confidence. Meetings increased, but decisions did not become clearer.

The visible request was for mapping or process support. The deeper issue was business-side clarity.

**What Changed**

The focus shifted from documenting the current process to clarifying the operating model the ERP system needed to support.

Leaders defined which workflows mattered most, who owned key decisions, what governance was needed, which data decisions had to be made, and what had to be stabilized in the next 90 days. Value stream mapping could still be useful, but it became an input to a broader leadership discussion rather than the entire intervention.

The question changed from, "Can we map the process?" to, "What business condition must the ERP system help us improve, and what decisions must leaders make before more configuration continues?"

**Result**

The organization gained a clearer path for the implementation. Rework was reduced, scope churn became easier to control, decision speed improved, and leaders had more confidence in the implementation path.

The value was not the map itself. The value was reducing confusion, clarifying ownership, improving decision quality, and aligning the system design with the business condition.

**Execution Reliability Lesson**

ERP problems are often described as technology problems when they are actually business-side clarity problems.

Before asking the software team to build, configure, or fix more, leaders should clarify the business condition, process ownership, decision rights, data expectations, governance, and success measures. The visible request may be a tool. The actual need may be operating architecture.

## Capacity Problems Deserve Diagnosis Before Capital

Capacity problems present a similar risk because the potential solutions are often expensive.

When an organization believes it does not have enough capacity, the natural response is to consider adding people, equipment, shifts, square footage, outsourcing, or even another facility. In some cases, those investments are necessary. There are times when the demand truly exceeds the capacity of the system, and the organization must invest.

However, the more money the organization is considering spending, the more careful it should be about understanding the condition.

Before adding cost structure, leaders should understand how the current capacity is being used. They should understand the constraint, the flow of work, the utilization losses, the rework, the downtime, the changeovers, the scheduling issues, the material shortages, and the decisions that affect throughput.

For example, an organization may believe it needs more equipment when the real issue is downtime, poor scheduling, or long changeovers. Another may believe it needs more space when the real issue is excess inventory or poor flow. Another may believe it needs more people when the real issue is rework, unclear priorities, or work waiting for decisions.

The point is not to avoid investment. The point is to make the right investment.

A capacity problem should not begin with the question, "What should we buy?" It should begin with a more disciplined set of questions:

1. What is the required output?
2. What is the current demonstrated output?
3. Where is the constraint?
4. What losses are reducing effective capacity?
5. What capacity can be recovered through better flow, stability, scheduling, quality, or changeover performance?
6. What investment is still needed after the current system is understood?

This is another reason to begin with the business condition. If leaders begin with the solution, they may add cost before they understand the system. If they begin with the condition, they can determine whether the best answer is operational improvement, capital investment, or some combination of both.

## The Role of Measures and Value

Starting with the business condition also requires measures and value.

If the organization cannot define how the condition will be measured, the improvement effort will be difficult to guide. If it cannot define the value of improvement, the work may not receive the attention and resources it needs.

Measures help answer the question: how will we know whether the condition improved?

Value helps answer the question: why does this matter?

For example, reducing lead time may improve customer responsiveness, reduce inventory, free cash, increase capacity, reduce expediting, and improve revenue recognition. Improving first-pass yield may reduce scrap, rework, delays, customer complaints, and quality risk. Improving project execution may reduce missed milestones, leadership escalation, resource conflict, and implementation risk.

The value may be financial, non-financial, or both. In many cases, the financial value is important, but the strategic value is also significant. Leaders may care about customer confidence, employee frustration, scalability, management bandwidth, or risk reduction.

This is why objectives, measures, and value are so important. They keep the work connected to the business.

Without them, the organization may complete the tool and still have a weak understanding of whether the work mattered.

## What This Means for Leaders

Leaders should be careful not to confuse familiarity with correctness. A familiar tool may feel like the safe answer, but it may not be the right answer. The best improvement work begins with disciplined inquiry.

This means leaders should be willing to pause before launching the initiative and ask:

1. What condition are we trying to improve?
2. Why does this condition matter now?
3. What result would be valuable?
4. How will we measure progress?
5. What is likely preventing the condition from improving today?
6. What leadership decisions or resources will be required?
7. What cadence will ensure follow-through?

These questions may slow the conversation briefly, but they usually speed up execution later. They reduce the chance that the organization will invest in activity that does not address the real constraint.

This also changes the role of the CI leader, functional leader, or improvement professional. The role is not simply to provide the requested method. The role is to help the organization connect the method to the business outcome.

That is where real value is created.

## Execution Reliability Check: Business Condition

If the business condition is weak or unclear, improvement work often begins with the method rather than the need. Leaders may approve training, mapping, kaizen events, daily management, or problem-solving work without a clear understanding of what operating condition must improve.

When this element is weak, the organization may see several symptoms:

- Improvement activity is visible, but business impact is unclear.
- Tools are selected because they are familiar rather than because they fit the condition.
- Teams complete workshops or training without changing performance.
- Leaders debate methods before agreeing on the problem.
- Success is measured by completion of activity rather than improvement in the business.

The leadership question is simple:

***What condition of the business must improve, and why does that condition matter now?***

Until that question is answered, the organization is not ready to begin with the tool.

Chapter 2 builds on this point by showing why execution often fails before the work begins. Once the business condition is clear, leaders still need agreement on objectives, measures, value, roles, decisions, resources, and cadence.

# Chapter 2: Execution Fails Before It Starts

Execution problems often show up late, but many of them are created early.

A project loses momentum. A training program produces limited application. A value stream map identifies important opportunities, but implementation stalls. An improvement initiative receives interest but does not move to a decision.

When this happens, it is natural to look for the problem in implementation. The team did not follow through. Leaders became distracted. Resources were not available. People returned to old habits.

Those explanations may be partly true, but through many years of experience, I have learned that the weakness was often built into the work before implementation began. The organization started before it had clear agreement on the objective, measures, value, decision process, resources, and follow-up cadence.

This is a common pattern in operational improvement, leadership initiatives, training programs, ERP readiness efforts, value stream mapping, and advisory work. The topic may be different, but the failure mode is similar. People agree that something should be done, but they have not agreed precisely enough on what should be different, how success will be measured, why the work matters, who owns the decision, and how progress will be reviewed.

When that agreement is missing, the work becomes vulnerable to drift.

The meetings, training, maps, and charters may still happen, but the foundation for execution is weak.

The issue is not always lack of interest. In many cases, leaders are interested. Sponsors are engaged. Participants are willing. The issue is that interest has not been converted into explicit agreement.

Execution requires more than interest. It requires clarity, ownership, measures, value, resources, and cadence.

## Where This Chapter Fits in the Execution Reliability Model

This chapter develops the second element of the Execution Reliability Model: objectives, measures, and value. Once leaders understand the business condition, they need enough agreement to begin the work intelligently.

Without this agreement, the organization can begin activity before it has the foundation required for execution. The work may start with interest, but interest alone is not enough to sustain commitment when tradeoffs appear.

Agreement does not mean every answer is known. It means leaders have clarified what should be different, how success will be measured, why the work matters, who owns key decisions, and how progress will be reviewed.

## Conceptual Agreement Before Action

Before beginning any significant improvement work, leaders should establish conceptual agreement.

Conceptual agreement includes explicit agreement on the business objectives, measures of success, value of improvement, general approach, roles, and decision path. It does not mean the team has solved the problem. It means the organization has enough shared understanding to begin the work intelligently.

Leaders should not launch an internal initiative until the key stakeholders have agreed on what will be different, how success will be determined, and why the work matters.

If leaders cannot state the objective clearly, the project team will struggle. If the measure is unclear, progress will be debated. If the value is weak, resources will be difficult to protect. If the decision path is unclear, the work will stall when tradeoffs are required. If follow-up is not scheduled, action items will drift.

Conceptual agreement does not guarantee success. It does, however, reduce the likelihood that the organization will confuse activity with execution.

A useful way to test agreement is to ask:

1. What are we trying to improve?
2. What will be different when this is successful?
3. How will we know it worked?
4. What value will be created?
5. Who owns the result?
6. Who must approve or resource the work?
7. When will we review progress and make decisions?

These questions are simple. The difficulty is in requiring clear answers before moving forward.

## In Practice: When Interest Was Mistaken for Readiness

### Situation

An operations leader wanted to begin an improvement effort because delivery performance had become inconsistent and several recurring process issues were consuming management attention. The need was real. The leader understood the operational pain, believed the work mattered, and expressed support for moving forward.

The early conversations were encouraging. The issue was relevant, the proposed work seemed useful, and the timing appeared reasonable. Everyone left the discussion believing the initiative was likely to move forward.

**Typical Response**

The typical response was to treat this interest as readiness. The organization began discussing dates, participants, scope, and content. Internal leaders started preparing communication. The CI leader or outside facilitator began shaping the approach.

This felt like progress because the conversation had moved from concern to action. However, several important execution questions remained unanswered.

**What Was Actually Happening**

The agreement was more apparent than real. The sponsor supported the idea, but the final decision owner had not committed. The budget was assumed, but not approved. The people required for the work were already assigned to other priorities. The organization had not agreed on what success would look like. The next review date was not scheduled. The sponsor could recommend the work, but could not fully approve or resource it.

In that situation, the issue was not lack of interest. The issue was that interest had not yet been converted into the conditions required for execution.

**What Changed**

Before launching the work, leaders tested startability. That meant clarifying several practical questions:

- Has the final decision owner agreed?
- Is the budget or resource path clear?
- Are the required participants available?
- What business condition will the work improve?
- What will success look like?
- Who owns the result?
- What decisions may be required?
- When will progress be reviewed?

These questions did not delay execution. They exposed the conditions required to support it.

**Result**
Once these questions were answered, the organization had a stronger foundation. The work had a clearer objective, a more reliable decision path, better sponsorship, and a defined review cadence.

Without that clarity, the work could have started with enthusiasm but drifted once tradeoffs, resource conflicts, or competing priorities appeared.

**Execution Reliability Lesson**
Interest is not the same as readiness. A leader can believe the work matters, and the organization can still lack the conditions required to begin and sustain it.

The practical point is to distinguish between agreement in principle and readiness to act. The first creates interest. The second creates execution.

## Objectives Must Be Stated in Business Terms

The first element is the objective.

An objective should describe what will be different in the business or operating condition. It should not simply describe the activity to be performed.

For example, "conduct value stream mapping" is not a strong objective. It describes an activity. A stronger objective might be to reduce order-to-ship lead time, improve delivery reliability, identify the constraints limiting capacity, reduce delays between engineering release and production, or improve cross-functional flow in a specific value stream.

"Train 20 Green Belts" is also not a complete objective. It describes participation. A stronger objective might be to develop internal problem-solving capability while completing projects that improve quality, delivery, productivity, or cost in targeted areas.

"Implement daily management" is not enough. The objective may be to make performance gaps visible earlier, improve escalation, reduce surprise, strengthen supervisor follow-through, or improve schedule adherence.

The distinction matters because activity-based objectives allow people to complete the work without improving the business condition.

If the objective is to hold a workshop, the workshop can be successful even if the business does not improve. If the objective is to reduce lead time or improve execution reliability, the workshop is only useful to the extent that it helps achieve that result.

This is why objectives should be stated in terms the business cares about. They may include lead time, productivity, quality, delivery, inventory, cash, capacity, customer responsiveness, risk, decision speed, employee capability, or management bandwidth.

The objective should answer the question: what condition are we trying to change?

## Measures Make Progress Visible

The second element is the measure.

Measures help the organization determine whether the condition is improving. Without measures, progress becomes subjective. People may feel that the effort is going well because meetings are happening, participants are engaged, or outputs are being produced. Those things may be positive, but they do not necessarily prove that the business condition is improving.

A useful measure does not need to be complicated. It should be clear enough to guide action and honest enough to reveal whether progress is real.

For example:

- If the objective is lead time reduction, the measure may be order-to-ship lead time, quote-to-order time, engineering release time, or total project cycle time.
- If the objective is delivery reliability, the measure may be on-time delivery, schedule adherence, missed commitments, or late-order backlog.
- If the objective is quality improvement, the measure may be defects, first-pass yield, rework, customer complaints, or cost of poor quality.
- If the objective is capacity improvement, the measure may be output per shift, utilization of the constraint, overtime, backlog, or available hours lost to downtime and changeover.
- If the objective is leadership execution, the measure may include action completion, escalation response time, decision cycle time, project milestone reliability, or the health of daily management routines.

The measure should also be connected to the level of the work. A project team needs measures it can influence. Executives need measures that show whether the business condition is changing. Both may be required.

A common mistake is to select measures that are easy to track but not useful for managing the work. Another mistake is to select measures that are so high-level that the team cannot tell whether its actions are helping.

Measures should create visibility, not confusion.

## Value Protects the Work

The third element is value.

Value answers the question: why does this matter?

If the value is unclear, the work will be difficult to protect when the business gets busy. Leaders may agree that the effort is worthwhile in principle, but when resources become constrained, customer issues arise, or competing priorities appear, the work may lose attention.

This is one reason many improvement efforts drift. The value was never made explicit enough to justify sustained focus.

Value can be financial or non-financial. Financial value may include cost reduction, margin improvement, revenue protection, inventory reduction, cash improvement, productivity gain, scrap reduction, reduced overtime, avoided capital, or faster revenue recognition.

Non-financial value may include customer confidence, employee frustration reduction, risk reduction, improved decision quality, better launch readiness, stronger leadership cadence, improved supplier performance, or greater scalability.

In many cases, the value includes both.

For example, reducing lead time may have financial value through lower inventory, less expediting, improved revenue timing, and better utilization of capacity. It may also have strategic value through improved customer responsiveness and reduced management firefighting.

Improving problem-solving capability may create value through completed projects, but it may also create value by reducing dependence on a few experts and improving the organization's ability to respond to future problems.

Strengthening daily management may not show up immediately as a single cost-reduction number, but it may reduce surprises, improve escalation, shorten response time, and create a more reliable operating system.

Leaders should be willing to discuss value before launching the work. This does not require false precision. It does require enough clarity to justify the investment of time, attention, and resources.

A useful question is: if we improve this condition, what value will be created or protected?

## Ownership and Decision Rights

The fourth element is ownership.

Many efforts stall because ownership is unclear. A sponsor may want the work to happen, but not own the result. A project leader may coordinate activity, but not have authority over the resources. A cross-functional team may identify improvements, but no one owns the decisions required to implement them.

This is especially common in work that crosses departments.

For example, a value stream improvement may require changes in sales, planning, purchasing, production, quality, and shipping. If no one owns the end-to-end result, each function may agree in principle but protect its own priorities in practice.

An ERP readiness effort may require business process decisions, data decisions, system configuration decisions, and governance decisions. If decision rights are unclear, the project team may continue meeting while key questions remain unresolved.

A training program may require participants to complete projects, but their managers may control their time and priorities. If managers do not own the application of learning, participants may struggle to make progress.

Ownership should be defined before the work begins.

This includes several questions:

1. Who owns the business result?
2. Who sponsors the work?
3. Who owns day-to-day execution?
4. Who controls the resources?
5. Who must approve changes?
6. Who resolves cross-functional tradeoffs?
7. Who will review progress?

These questions may reveal that the organization is not ready to begin. That is useful information. It is better to discover weak ownership before launching than after the work has stalled.

## Startability Is Different from Interest

One of the most important tests before beginning an initiative is startability.

By startability, I mean the organization's real ability to begin and support the work. Interest is not the same as startability. A leader may be interested. A sponsor may be enthusiastic. A team may agree that the issue matters. But the conditions are not yet in place to begin the work.

Startability includes practical conditions such as:

- Funding or budget logic
- Leadership sponsorship
- Available participants
- Access to data
- Decision rights
- Resource availability
- Timing
- Administrative path
- Implementation authority
- Review cadence

Interest becomes startability only when the practical conditions are in place: objective, measure, value, ownership, resources, decision path, and review cadence.

# Figure 3. The Startability Test

*Execution requires more than interest.*

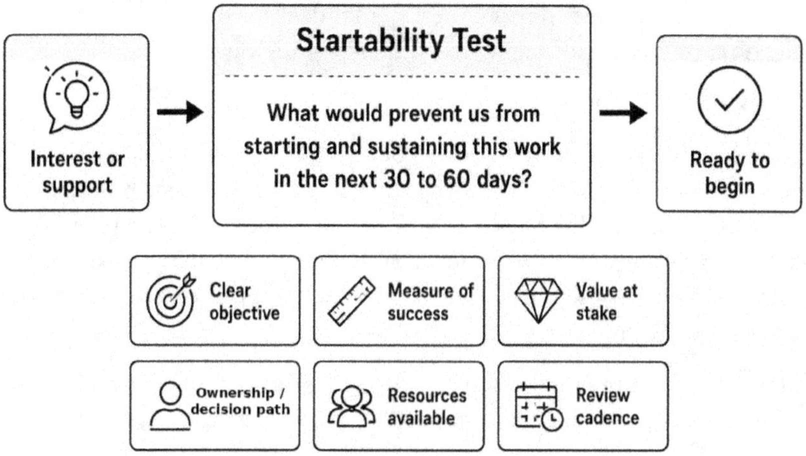


*Startability is different from interest.*

### Leadership Application

*Use Figure 3 before committing resources or announcing a launch. The point is not to delay action; it is to expose the conditions that will make action difficult to sustain. If several checklist items are unclear, the next step is not a larger rollout. It is a tighter startability discussion.*

Without these things in place, trouble is inevitable. A department launches a project before resources are available. A team agrees to improve a process before decision rights are clear. Leaders approve training before project sponsorship is defined. A future-state map is created before the organization is prepared to implement.

In each case, the interest is real, but the conditions are not yet in place to begin the work.

A useful question is: what would prevent us from starting and sustaining this work in the next 30 to 60 days?

The answer often reveals important constraints.

## The Follow-Up Cadence Must Be Established Early

The fifth element is follow-up cadence.

Many organizations make the mistake of beginning work without scheduling the decision points needed to sustain it. A team may agree to act, but no one determines when progress will be reviewed. A project plan may be created, but no meeting is scheduled to make the required decisions. A workshop may produce action items, but the review cadence is unclear.

When follow-up is not built into the work, drift becomes likely.

A follow-up cadence does not need to be complicated. It should fit the nature of the work. A daily management issue may need daily review. A project may need weekly or biweekly review. A value stream implementation plan may need weekly team review and monthly leadership review. A training-based project may need review between sessions. An externally supported effort may need a monthly executive review.

The key is to build the review rhythm into the work before attention begins to drift. Do not launch work and hope that attention remains.

The follow-up cadence should answer:

1. When will progress be reviewed?
2. Who must attend?
3. What decisions may be required?
4. What information will be reviewed?
5. How will barriers be escalated?
6. What happens if actions are not completed?

Follow-up is not an administrative detail. It is part of execution design.

## Why Vague Agreement Creates Drift

Many initiatives begin with vague agreement.

People agree that the organization should improve. They agree that lead time is too long, quality should be better, employees need training, daily management would help, or the ERP implementation needs more clarity. These statements may all be true, but they are not specific enough to guide execution.

Vague agreement feels good in the beginning because it avoids difficult conversations. No one has to make tradeoffs. No one has to define measures. No one has to commit resources. No one has to clarify authority. No one has to say what will not be done.

The problem appears later.

When the team needs a decision, the agreement is not strong enough. When resources are required, the value is not clear enough. When a measure is reviewed, people debate what success means. When a cross-functional conflict appears, no one knows who owns the tradeoff. When the work slows down, there is no cadence to bring it back into focus.

Vague agreement creates polite beginnings and difficult endings.

It is better to have the difficult conversation early.

## The Role of a Smaller First Phase

A smaller first phase can be useful when the need appears real but readiness is incomplete.

This might include an executive clarity sprint, operational assessment, value stream diagnostic, ERP readiness review, project selection session, or leadership alignment workshop.

A smaller first phase can help answer:

1. What is the real business condition?
2. What value is at stake?
3. Who owns the decision?
4. What constraints must be addressed?
5. What scope is realistic?
6. What resources are required?
7. What should the next phase include?

This approach is useful when the organization is interested but not yet aligned. It can prevent leaders from launching a large effort before the decision system is ready to support it.

However, a smaller first phase should not become a way to avoid the value conversation. It should still have clear objectives, measures, value, timing, and follow-up. Otherwise, it will suffer from the same problem as the larger effort.

The first phase must also be real work. It should create useful insight and help the organization make a better decision. It should not become another activity disconnected from a clear decision path.

## What This Means for Internal Leaders

Before launching an initiative, internal leaders should test whether the work is anchored in a real business condition, supported by clear objectives and measures, connected to value, owned by the right leader, resourced through a clear decision path, and supported by a review cadence. If those conditions are not in place, the initiative should not be started.

## Execution Reliability Check: Startability

Before beginning significant improvement work, leaders can use a simple pre-execution check:

1. What business condition are we trying to improve?
2. What will be different if we succeed?
3. How will success be measured?
4. What value will be created or protected?
5. Who owns the business result?
6. Who must approve or resource the work?
7. What decisions or tradeoffs are likely to be required?
8. Can the work be started in the next 30 to 60 days?
9. What could prevent implementation?
10. When is the next review or decision meeting already scheduled?

The last question is important. If the next review is not scheduled, the organization has not fully designed the execution path.

Chapter 3 extends the logic from agreement to system view. Even when objectives and measures are clear, leaders must understand the flow of work across functions before they optimize individual parts of the organization.

# Chapter 3: See the Whole System Before Optimizing the Parts

Most organizations are managed by departments, functions, and reporting relationships.

Sales has its metrics. Operations has its metrics. Engineering has its metrics. Quality has its metrics. Finance has its metrics. Each group may be working hard and improving its own performance.

However, customers do not experience the organization by department. They experience the flow of work across the organization: the time required to receive a product, service, decision, answer, approval, shipment, quote, design, or resolution. They experience the handoffs, waiting, rework, errors, delays, and communication gaps between functions.

This is why leaders must see the whole system before optimizing the parts. A function can improve its own performance and still fail to improve the customer experience or business result. In some cases, local improvement can make the overall system worse because the work is being optimized in the wrong place or in the wrong sequence.

Functional performance still matters. Functions need competence, standards, capacity, and accountability. But functional performance must be understood in the context of the larger system that delivers value.

By system, I mean the connected flow of work, information, decisions, materials, approvals, resources, and follow-up required to produce a result. In a manufacturing environment, this may include order entry, planning, purchasing, production, quality, shipping, and customer service. In a service environment, it may include intake, evaluation, approval, scheduling, delivery, billing, and follow-up. In an engineering or product development environment, it may include concept development, design, testing, review, regulatory input, supplier involvement, transfer to production, and launch.

The form of the work changes by industry, but the principle is the same. Value is created through a system. If leaders cannot see the system, they will often improve the wrong things.

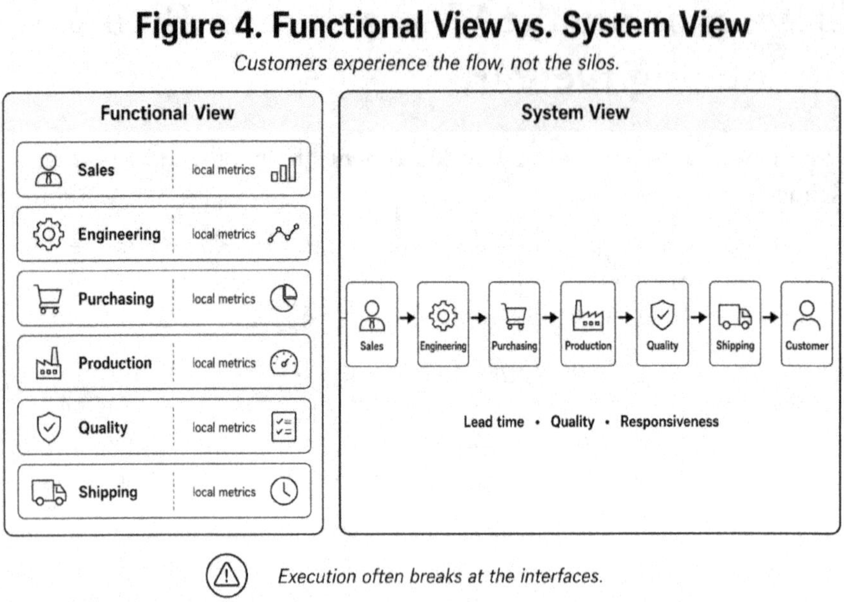


### Leadership Application

*Use Figure 4 when performance looks acceptable inside each function but the customer still experiences delay, rework, or poor responsiveness. The leadership question is not only which department is performing. It is where the flow of work, information, decisions, and follow-up breaks down between departments.*

## Where This Chapter Fits in the Execution Reliability Model

This chapter addresses the system view element of the Execution Reliability Model. A business condition is rarely produced by one department alone. It is usually produced by the way work moves across functions, decisions, systems, and handoffs.

Leaders improve execution reliability when they understand the system before optimizing its parts. Without that view, they may improve a local metric while leaving the business condition unchanged. In my work with leadership teams, this is one of the hardest shifts to make: moving from asking how each function is performing to asking how the work is actually flowing across functions.

The system view also prepares the organization for better problem solving. Chapter 4 will focus on the discipline required to define and solve problems in the context of the actual work.

## The Problem with Local Optimization

Local optimization occurs when one function improves its own performance in a way that does not improve, and may even harm, the overall value stream.

This happens frequently because most organizations measure and manage performance functionally. Purchasing may be measured on purchase price. Production may be measured on efficiency. Engineering may be measured on design milestones. Quality may be measured on inspection results. Customer service may be measured on response time. Each metric may make sense in isolation, but the combined effect may not improve the total business condition.

For example, purchasing may reduce component cost by buying in larger quantities or switching suppliers. The purchase price looks better, but inventory increases, quality problems appear, lead time grows, or engineering support increases because the supplier does not fully understand the requirements.

Production may increase efficiency by running larger batches. The department's productivity may improve, but downstream areas receive too much inventory, changeovers become harder to schedule, defects are discovered later, and customer responsiveness declines.

Engineering may complete a design milestone on time, but unresolved manufacturability issues are pushed downstream. The project appears to be on schedule until production, quality, or suppliers begin discovering problems that should have been addressed earlier.

In each case, the function may be doing what it was asked to do. The problem is that the measures and routines did not force the organization to consider the entire flow of work.

This is not a people problem. It is usually a system-design problem.

## Value Stream Thinking

Value stream thinking is one of the most useful ways to help leaders see the system.

A value stream includes the actions required to bring a product, service, or deliverable from request to completion. It includes both the work that directly creates value and the work that supports, delays, transfers, inspects, approves, corrects, or manages the flow.

The purpose of value stream thinking is not simply to create a map. The purpose is to understand how work actually flows and where the major opportunities exist.

A value stream view helps leaders see several things that are often hidden in functional reporting:

- How long work waits between steps.
- Where information is incomplete or incorrect.
- Where handoffs create delay or confusion.
- Where batches are created.
- Where rework occurs.
- Where decisions are delayed.
- Where inventory or backlog accumulates.
- Where ownership is unclear.
- Where the customer is affected.

These issues are often not visible in a departmental review. Each function may report that it is doing its part, while the overall lead time remains too long or the customer experience remains poor.

Value stream thinking changes the question. Instead of asking only, "How is each department performing?" leaders begin to ask, "How is the work flowing through the system?"

That is a different level of management.

## Mapping Is a Means, Not the Objective

Value stream mapping is a useful method, but the map is not the objective.

A current-state map can help the organization understand how work flows today. A future-state map can help the organization define a better way for work to flow. These are valuable outputs. However, they do not create improvement by themselves.

The value comes from what the organization learns and what it is willing to do with that learning.

This is a common failure point. A team holds a value stream mapping workshop. Participants identify delays, bottlenecks, rework, poor handoffs, excess inventory, unclear information, and opportunities for improvement. The group creates a future-state map and an implementation plan. The workshop feels successful.

Then the work slows down.

The actions require decisions from leaders who were not fully involved. The improvements cross functional boundaries. Resources are needed. Some changes affect metrics or incentives. Some require changes to scheduling, staffing, supplier expectations, engineering priorities, or information systems. The team realizes that the map exposed issues the organization is not yet prepared to address.

In that case, the mapping method did its job. The management system did not.

A value stream map should not be treated as a deliverable to file away. It should be treated as a decision-making tool. It should help leaders understand what must change in the operating system.

If leaders are not prepared to act on what the map reveals, the organization should not expect mapping alone to improve performance.

## In Practice: When the Map Revealed a Cross-Functional Ownership Gap

**Situation**
A medical device manufacturer requested a value stream mapping workshop because lead time was too long and delivery performance was inconsistent. The request was reasonable. The process crossed several departments, and leaders believed the team needed to see the flow of work more clearly so it could identify waste and create a better future state.

Each department understood its own portion of the work. Sales or customer service understood the customer request. Planning understood the schedule. Operations understood the production constraints. Quality understood the inspection and release points. Shipping understood the final delivery issues.

However, no one had a complete view of the total flow.

**Typical Response**
The typical response was to conduct the mapping workshop, identify delays, create a current-state map, design a future-state map, and develop an implementation plan. That work was useful. It helped the team see handoffs, queues, rework, incomplete information, and other sources of delay.

The workshop felt productive because important issues became visible and the team identified practical improvement opportunities.

**What Was Actually Happening**
The mapping discussion showed that the work was not delayed by one obvious

bottleneck. It was delayed by a series of handoffs, queues, clarifications, and decisions that occurred between functions. Information was not always complete when it moved to the next step. Some work waited for approval. Some work started before requirements were clear. Some problems were discovered late because the process relied on inspection or review after the fact.

The current-state map was useful because it made these conditions visible. However, the more important discovery was that no one clearly owned the end-to-end value stream. Each function was managing its part, but no leader or routine was managing the flow across the whole system.

The problem was not only waste in the process. It was a cross-functional ownership gap.

**What Changed**

As the team developed the future state, leaders clarified the management questions that the map had exposed:

- Who owns the cross-functional process?
- Which measures will be used to manage the total flow?
- What handoff requirements need to be standardized?
- Which decisions need to be made earlier?
- What issues should be escalated, and to whom?
- How will the implementation plan be reviewed after the workshop?

These questions could not be answered by the map alone. They required leadership ownership and operating cadence.

**Result**

The value stream map became more than a process picture. It became a decision-making tool. Leaders could see where the system was breaking down, where ownership was unclear, and where the organization needed a better way to manage flow across functions.

The work moved from identifying waste to improving the management system around the value stream.

**Execution Reliability Lesson**

A value stream map does not only show process problems. It can also reveal management problems.

When the map exposes unclear ownership, delayed decisions, weak handoffs, or missing cadence, the organization should not treat the issue as a mapping problem. The map has done its job. The next requirement is leadership ownership of the cross-functional system.

## Client Example: When the Constraint Moved to the Interface

**Situation**
A global biopharmaceutical organization improved reliability, predictability, and throughput in its supply chain function. The work produced meaningful gains, but as the function improved, the next constraint became more visible.

**What Was Actually Happening**
The limiting issue was no longer only within supply chain. It had moved to the interface between R&D and production. Products moving toward commercialization were delayed by misaligned priorities, unclear ownership, deferred decisions, and repeated handoffs among R&D, Technical Operations, Quality, and Supply Chain.

**Result**
The organization learned that once local performance improves, the next constraint may appear at the enterprise interface. Each function did not need to optimize harder in isolation. Leaders needed to manage the points where value, risk, and accountability crossed functional boundaries.

**Execution Reliability Lesson**
This is the system view in practice. Improvement in one function can reveal the next constraint in the broader operating system. When that happens, leaders must shift attention from local optimization to enterprise integration.

## Seeing Waiting as a Business Cost

One of the most important things a value stream view reveals is waiting.

Waiting is often thought of as a shop-floor form of waste: people waiting for material, machines waiting for operators, or products waiting between steps. That is important, but waiting is much broader than that.

In many organizations, work waits for information. It waits for approvals. It waits for decisions. It waits for clarification. It waits for engineering input, quality review, supplier response, customer feedback, management direction, or system updates.

This waiting may not look expensive because people are still busy. The department appears active. Meetings are being held. Emails are being sent. People are working on other tasks while the item waits.

But the waiting still has a cost.

It increases lead time. It creates expediting. It delays revenue. It increases work-in-process or backlog. It causes people to switch tasks. It creates frustration for customers and employees. It hides problems until later. It forces managers to spend time following up, clarifying, and escalating.

Waiting is especially expensive when it occurs at decision points. A project may wait for a decision that no one clearly owns. A customer issue may wait for approval to deviate from the normal process. An ERP implementation may wait for the business to define a workflow. A supplier problem may wait for engineering, quality, and purchasing to agree on the response.

The organization may describe these as communication issues, but they are often decision-system issues.

When leaders look at the whole system, they can begin to see waiting as a business cost rather than as an unavoidable inconvenience.

## Interfaces Are Where Execution Often Breaks

Execution often breaks at the interfaces.

An interface or handoff is a point where work, information, accountability, or decision-making moves from one person, group, function, system, or organization to another. Examples include sales to operations, engineering to manufacturing, purchasing to suppliers, quality to production, operations to customer service, or leadership to project teams.

Interfaces are important because they are places where assumptions become visible.

One group believes it has completed its work, but the next group does not have what it needs. One function assumes another function owns the decision. One team believes a requirement is clear, while another interprets it differently. One metric rewards speed, while another rewards caution. One department measures completion, while another experiences rework.

These interface problems can consume a significant amount of management attention. They produce follow-up meetings, clarifying emails, escalation, rework, missed commitments, and frustration.

In many organizations, the problem is not that people are unwilling to cooperate. The problem is that the system does not clearly define what must be transferred, when, in what condition, with what decision rights, and with what follow-up.

This is why cross-functional improvement requires leadership involvement. The people doing the work may see the problem, but they may not have the authority to change the interface. Leaders must clarify ownership, expectations, measures, and escalation paths across the boundary.

If leaders do not manage the interfaces, the organization will continue to lose value between functions.

## The Extended Value Stream

In some cases, the system extends beyond the organization itself.

Suppliers, contract manufacturers, distributors, customers, logistics providers, regulatory bodies, and technology partners may all influence performance. The value stream may include several organizations, not just several departments.

This is especially important in supply chain, product development, healthcare, aerospace, medical devices, biopharma, and other regulated or complex environments. A company may work hard to improve its internal process while a major constraint exists at a supplier, a customer handoff, a regulatory review point, or a third-party service provider.

If leaders look only inside their own walls, they may miss the real constraint.

For example, an organization may reduce internal production lead time, but total lead time remains long because suppliers require extended replenishment time or customers frequently change requirements. A company may improve internal design review, but launch delays continue because supplier capability was not considered early enough. A healthcare process may improve internal scheduling, but patient flow still suffers because external approvals or discharge arrangements are delayed.

The extended value stream does not mean the organization can control everything. It means leaders must understand how external dependencies affect the business condition they are trying to improve.

In many cases, improvement requires better alignment with suppliers, customers, or partners. This may include clearer requirements, better forecasting, joint problem solving, shared measures, stronger review cadence, or different commercial agreements. I addressed this topic in detail in an earlier book, *Improving the Extended Value Stream*, published by Productivity Press in 2006.

The broader point is simple: the system that produces the result may be larger than the organization chart.

## Avoiding Islands of Excellence

One risk in improvement work is creating islands of excellence.

An island of excellence is a department, cell, team, or process area that improves locally while the larger system remains disconnected. The area may look good, the board may be well maintained, the process may be more stable, and the team may be engaged. But the improvement does not translate into a meaningful change in the customer experience or business performance.

This can happen when improvement work is selected based on convenience rather than system impact. It can also happen when leaders reward local activity more than value-stream results.

For example, a production cell may improve internal flow, but orders still wait for engineering release, material availability, inspection, or shipment. A purchasing team may reduce price, but total cost increases because of quality or delivery problems. An administrative team may reduce processing time, but the customer still waits because the approval step did not change.

The local improvement may still have value, but leaders should be clear about what it does and does not improve.

To avoid islands of excellence, leaders should ask:

1. What business condition are we trying to improve?
2. Where is the constraint in the total flow?
3. Will this improvement change the customer or business outcome?
4. What upstream or downstream changes are required?
5. Which functions must be involved?
6. How will we measure value-stream performance?

These questions help keep improvement focused on the system, not only on the part.

## The Role of Leadership in System-Level Improvement

System-level improvement requires leadership because many of the most important issues cross boundaries.

Teams can identify problems. They can improve work within their control. They can test countermeasures and recommend changes. But many value stream problems require leadership decisions about priorities, resources, ownership, measures, and tradeoffs.

For example, reducing lead time may require smaller batches, different scheduling rules, supplier changes, cross-training, quality-at-the-source, engineering support, and different performance metrics. No single department may have the authority to make all of those changes.

This is why leaders must be involved before, during, and after system-level improvement work: clarifying the business condition and value at stake, removing barriers and making decisions during the work, and reviewing progress so the implementation plan does not drift.

When leaders are absent, system-level improvement often becomes analysis without execution.

When leaders are involved, the organization has a better chance of converting insight into action.

## Designing Improvement Around the System

If leaders want to improve the system, the improvement effort should be designed around the system.

This means selecting the right scope. A scope that is too narrow may miss the real constraint. A scope that is too broad may become unmanageable. The right scope is large enough to see the important flow and small enough to act.

It also means involving the right people. A value stream effort should include people who understand the work, people who provide information or resources, and leaders who can make decisions. If key functions are missing, the team may create recommendations that cannot be implemented.

It means using the right measures. Department-level measures are not enough. The organization needs measures that reflect value-stream performance, such as lead time, on-time delivery, first-pass yield, inventory, backlog, customer response, or project completion reliability.

It means creating an implementation plan. A future-state map without implementation is only a drawing. The plan should include actions, owners, due dates, measures, review cadence, and escalation paths.

Finally, it means managing follow-through. The organization should expect obstacles. Some countermeasures will need to be adjusted. Some assumptions will be wrong. Some support will be required from functions not fully represented in the original work. This is normal. The management cadence is what keeps the work moving.

## Execution Reliability Check: System View

Before launching a major improvement effort, leaders can use a simple system-view check:

1. What business condition are we trying to improve?
2. What is the value stream or flow of work that produces this condition?
3. Where does the work begin and end?
4. Which functions, systems, suppliers, or customers influence the outcome?
5. Where does work wait, loop back, or get reworked?
6. Where are decisions delayed or revisited?
7. Which measures reflect total system performance?
8. Are we improving the constraint or only improving a visible local issue?
9. Who owns the value stream or cross-functional result?
10. What cadence will ensure that the future state is implemented?

These questions help leaders avoid the common mistake of optimizing the part while the whole system remains unchanged.

Chapter 4 continues this progression by moving from seeing the system to solving problems within it. Once leaders can see the flow of work, they need a disciplined way to define gaps, understand causes, and test countermeasures.

# Chapter 4: Problem Solving Is an Operating Discipline, Not a Form

Most organizations say they want better problem solving.

They want people to find root causes, use data, prevent recurrence, and stop jumping to solutions. They want fewer repeat problems, less firefighting, better decisions, and more ownership at the appropriate level of the organization.

Those are appropriate objectives. However, many organizations misunderstand what problem solving really requires.

They introduce a form, template, or methodology and assume the discipline will follow. They ask people to complete an A3, fill out a root cause analysis form, use 5 Whys, follow DMAIC, or document corrective actions. These methods can be very useful. In many cases, they provide the structure people need.

But the form is not the discipline.

Problem solving is the way an organization defines problems, understands current conditions, identifies causes, tests countermeasures, learns from results, and prevents recurrence. A form can help organize that thinking, but it cannot substitute for the thinking.

This distinction matters because organizations can become very good at completing forms without becoming very good at solving problems. A team can fill out an A3 and still have a weak problem statement. A corrective action report can be completed without identifying the real cause. A project can move through DMAIC phases while the team avoids the difficult facts.

When this happens, the organization has documentation, but not necessarily learning.

## Where This Chapter Fits in the Execution Reliability Model

This chapter develops the problem-solving discipline element of the Execution Reliability Model. When a business condition is clear and the system is visible, leaders still need a reliable way to understand and close the gap between current condition and target condition.

Forms, templates, and methodologies can help, but the real discipline is in how the organization defines problems, sees facts, investigates causes, tests countermeasures, learns from results, and prevents recurrence.

This discipline also connects directly to capability building. Chapter 5 will discuss why training only creates value when people apply the learning to real work with coaching, feedback, and reinforcement.

## What Is a Problem?

Let us begin with a simple definition.

***A problem is the gap between the current condition and the target condition or standard.***

This definition is important because it forces clarity. Without a clear gap, the organization may be working on a concern, complaint, symptom, preference, or solution idea rather than a problem.

For example, "we need more people" is not a problem statement. It may be a proposed solution. The problem may be that output is 20 percent below the level required to meet customer demand. The cause may involve staffing, but it may also involve downtime, quality losses, poor scheduling, long changeovers, material shortages, or unclear work methods.

"Employees do not follow the process" is also not a strong problem statement. It may reflect a concern, but it does not define the gap. A better starting point would be to identify which process standard is not being followed, how often the deviation occurs, where it occurs, what impact it has, and what conditions make the deviation more likely.

"Customers are unhappy" may be true, but it is too broad. The organization needs to understand what customers are experiencing. Are orders late? Are responses slow? Are defects increasing? Are invoices inaccurate? Are commitments unclear? Each of those problems would require a different investigation.

A clear problem statement helps the organization focus. It defines what is happening, where it is happening, when it is happening, how large the gap is, and why it matters.

Without that clarity, problem solving becomes vulnerable to opinion.

## The Rush to Solutions

One of the most common problem-solving failures is the rush to solutions.

This happens for understandable reasons. Leaders want action. Customers may be waiting. Employees may be frustrated. The issue may have occurred before. Someone may believe the cause is obvious. A solution may already be available.

In many organizations, people are rewarded for speed and decisiveness, not for carefully understanding the problem.

The problem is that fast action is not always effective action.

When teams jump to solutions too quickly, they often treat symptoms rather than causes. They add inspection instead of preventing the defect. They add meetings instead of clarifying ownership. They add expediting instead of fixing flow. They add training instead of improving the work method. They add headcount instead of addressing downtime, rework, or scheduling variation.

Some of these actions may help temporarily. In fact, containment is often necessary. If a customer is affected, the organization may need to take immediate action to protect the customer. If a safety issue exists, the organization must respond immediately. If production is stopped, the team may need to restore flow quickly.

I understand the pressure to move quickly; leaders often need containment immediately. But I have also seen how quickly containment becomes the substitute for real problem solving. After several years, multiple layers of checking and inspection have been installed while problems still recur.

However, containment is not the same as problem solving. Both may be necessary, but they should not be confused.

## Containment and Problem Solving

Containment and problem solving are both important, but they serve different purposes.

| Containment | Problem Solving |
|---|---|
| Protects the customer, patient, process, or schedule now. | Prevents recurrence by addressing the cause. |
| Often requires immediate action. | Requires understanding the current condition. |
| May include inspection, sorting, expediting, rework, or temporary process controls. | Uses facts, observation, data, and cause analysis. |
| Stabilizes the situation. | Changes the process or system that allowed the issue to occur. |
| Should not be mistaken for permanent improvement. | Should be checked for effectiveness and standardized if successful. |

In regulated or customer-sensitive environments, containment may be essential. The organization may need to protect the customer or process before the cause is fully understood. However, if containment becomes the only response, the same problems will continue to return.

The practical question is:

*Are we taking action to protect the customer now, or are we changing the process so the problem is less likely to recur?*

In many cases, both are needed.

## In Practice: When Quick Fixes Became the Management System

**Situation**
A mid-market manufacturer was experiencing recurring quality and delivery problems in one of its production areas. The team was working hard, and leaders were involved. When a problem occurred, the response was immediate. Supervisors expedited material, managers held short meetings, operators were reminded of the correct method, and quality added extra checks when needed.

On the surface, this looked like responsiveness.

**Typical Response**
The typical response was to keep reacting quickly. A late order triggered expediting. A defect triggered retraining. A missed handoff triggered another reminder. A documentation error triggered another inspection step.

Each response made sense in the moment. The customer needed to be protected, the schedule needed to recover, and leaders wanted to show urgency.

However, the same issues continued to return.

**What Was Actually Happening**
The organization had developed a quick-fix system rather than a problem-solving system. The responses were fast, but they were not changing the conditions that allowed the problems to recur.

When the team began looking more carefully at the current condition, the problems were not all the same. Some defects were related to unclear work instructions. Some delays were related to material not being available at the point of use. Some errors occurred during shift-to-shift handoffs. Some quality issues were more likely when production volume increased and supervisors were pulled into expediting.

The earlier responses treated these issues as if they were mainly behavior problems. The improved problem-solving effort showed that many of them were process and management-system problems.

**What Changed**
The organization changed both the countermeasures and the leadership questions.

Instead of relying primarily on reminders and retraining, the team clarified the work standard, changed how material was staged, improved the handoff process, and created a simple review of recurring abnormalities.

Leaders also changed the way they responded to problems. Instead of asking only who missed the step or when the order would be recovered, they began asking:

- What condition allowed the problem to occur?
- What facts do we have from the process?
- Is this an isolated abnormality or a recurring pattern?
- What support is needed to prevent recurrence?
- How will we know whether the countermeasure worked?

This shifted the discussion from reaction to learning.

**Result**
The organization still responded quickly when customers, quality, or delivery were at risk. That urgency remained necessary.

The difference was that urgency no longer substituted for problem solving. Recurring issues were studied more carefully, countermeasures were connected to causes, and leaders began to see patterns that were previously hidden by expediting, reminders, and extra checks.

**Execution Reliability Lesson**
Responsiveness is important, but responsiveness alone does not create execution reliability.

When every issue is treated as an isolated event, the organization becomes very good at reacting while the same process conditions remain in place. Problem solving improves when leaders stop treating repeated issues as one-off failures and begin looking for the system conditions behind them.

## Understanding the Current Condition

Good problem solving begins with understanding the current condition.

This means going beyond opinion, memory, and assumptions. The team needs to understand what is actually happening in the process. This may require observation, data collection, process review, interviews, document review, or direct study of the work.

In Lean terminology, we often say that leaders and teams should go to the gemba, the real place where the work occurs. The point is not to use Japanese terminology. The point is to see reality.

Many problems are misunderstood because people discuss them too far from the work. They meet in a conference room, review summary data, rely on secondhand explanations, and then develop a countermeasure. The discussion may sound logical, but it may be disconnected from the actual process conditions.

For example, a team may believe that operators are not following standard work. Observation may show that the standard is outdated, the material is not available in the expected location, the tools are difficult to access, or the work sequence does not match the actual demand pattern.

A manager may believe that a project team is missing deadlines because of poor accountability. Further review may show that the team is waiting for decisions from another function, working with unclear requirements, or trying to manage too many priorities at the same time.

A leader may believe that customer service response time is slow because employees are not working with urgency. Observation may show that employees are waiting for information from operations, engineering, finance, or a supplier before they can respond accurately.

In each case, the problem looks different when viewed from the work.

Understanding the current condition does not need to be overly complicated. The team can begin with practical questions:

1. What is the standard or expectation?
2. What is actually happening?
3. Where is the gap occurring?
4. How often does it occur?
5. When does it occur?
6. Who or what is affected?
7. What facts have we observed directly?
8. What assumptions are we making?

These questions help separate fact from opinion.

## Root Cause Thinking

Root cause analysis is often discussed but frequently misunderstood.

The purpose of root cause thinking is not to find someone to blame. It is to understand the process conditions that allowed the problem to occur. In many cases, the most useful causes are not personal causes, but system causes.

For example, "operator error" is usually not a sufficient root cause. An operator may have made an error, but the next question is why the system allowed the error to occur. Was the work method unclear? Was the training insufficient? Was the part difficult to distinguish from another part? Was the information incomplete? Was the person interrupted? Was the process designed in a way that made the error likely?

Similarly, "poor communication" is rarely a useful final cause. It may describe a symptom, but it does not usually explain what should change. The organization needs to understand what information was missing, where it should have been communicated, who needed it, when it was needed, and what mechanism failed.

Root cause thinking requires persistence. It asks the organization to move beyond the first explanation.

5 Whys can be helpful when used properly. The value is not in asking "why" exactly five times. The value is in moving from the visible symptom to the underlying process conditions. Fishbone diagrams, cause-and-effect analysis, Pareto analysis, process mapping, data stratification, and other methods can also help.

The method should fit the problem. A simple problem may require only a short investigation and a clear countermeasure. A complex problem may require data analysis, cross-functional review, experimentation, and leadership decisions.

The test of root cause analysis is not whether a tool was used. The test is whether the identified cause explains the problem and leads to an effective countermeasure.

## Countermeasures, Not Just Solutions

In continuous improvement work, the word countermeasure is often more useful than solution.

A solution can imply that the answer is final. A countermeasure suggests that the action is intended to address a cause and should be checked for effectiveness. This creates a more scientific mindset.

A countermeasure should be linked to the cause. If the cause is unclear, the countermeasure is likely to be weak. If the countermeasure does not address the cause, the problem may return.

For example, if a defect occurs because two similar parts are difficult to distinguish, retraining employees may not be enough. A better countermeasure may involve part presentation, visual differentiation, error-proofing, labeling, or changes to the work sequence.

If late project decisions are caused by unclear decision rights, adding another status meeting may not solve the problem. A better countermeasure may involve clarifying who owns specific decisions, when escalation should occur, and what information is required for approval.

If daily huddles are not improving performance because leaders do not respond to escalated issues, changing the board layout will not be enough. The countermeasure may need to address leader standard work, escalation expectations, and review cadence.

Countermeasures should be practical, testable, and connected to the cause. They should also include a way to determine whether they worked.

## PDCA as a Learning Cycle

Plan-Do-Check-Act, or PDCA, is one of the most useful ways to think about problem solving.

The Plan step includes defining the problem, understanding the current condition, identifying likely causes, and selecting countermeasures. The Do step involves implementing the countermeasure, often on a limited or controlled basis when possible. The Check step determines whether the countermeasure produced the expected result. The Act step standardizes the change if it worked or adjusts the approach if it did not.

The value of PDCA is that it treats improvement as learning.

Many organizations are comfortable with Plan and Do. They define an action and implement it. They are less disciplined with Check and Act. They do not always verify whether the action worked. They do not always standardize the improved method. They do not always adjust based on what was learned.

When Check and Act are weak, the organization becomes good at activity but poor at learning.

For example, a team may implement a new scheduling process, but fail to check whether schedule adherence improved. A supervisor may retrain employees, but not verify whether the error rate decreased. A project team may launch a new review process, but not evaluate whether decisions are being made faster.

In each case, action occurred. Learning may not have occurred.

PDCA helps prevent this. It reminds the organization that the countermeasure is a hypothesis. We believe this action will improve the condition because we believe this cause is contributing to the problem. After implementation, we need to check whether that belief was correct.

That is the discipline.

## A3 Thinking

A3 thinking is one way to structure problem solving. The A3 format typically includes the background, current condition, problem statement, target condition, root cause analysis, countermeasures, implementation plan, results, and follow-up.

The strength of A3 thinking is that it forces the team to tell the problem-solving story clearly and concisely. It also provides a useful coaching structure. A leader or coach can review the A3 and ask whether the problem is clear, whether the current condition is supported by facts, whether the root causes are logical, whether the countermeasures address the causes, and whether the results have been checked.

However, A3 thinking can be misused.

If the A3 becomes a form to complete after decisions have already been made, it loses much of its value. If leaders review the A3 only for format, they may miss the quality of the reasoning.

The A3 should be a thinking process, not an administrative document.

A useful A3 review should ask:

1. Is the problem clearly defined?
2. Is the current condition understood?
3. Is the target condition measurable?
4. Do the causes explain the gap?
5. Do the countermeasures address the causes?
6. Is the implementation plan realistic?
7. How will results be checked?
8. What did the team learn?

These questions help keep the focus on problem solving rather than form completion.

## DMAIC and Structured Projects

DMAIC is another structured problem-solving method. It is often used in Six Sigma and Lean Six Sigma project work. The phases are Define, Measure, Analyze, Improve, and Control.

Define clarifies the problem, objective, scope, customer impact, and business case. Measure establishes the current performance and data foundation. Analyze identifies causes. Improve develops and tests countermeasures. Control sustains the gains and prevents regression.

DMAIC is especially useful for problems that require project discipline, data analysis, cross-functional work, or a more rigorous improvement process.

However, DMAIC can become bureaucratic if the organization treats the phases as paperwork rather than as a disciplined way to learn. The project should not move from phase to phase simply because the slides are complete. It should move because the team has learned enough to justify the next step.

For example, a project should not leave Define if the problem is still vague. It should not leave Measure if the team does not understand current performance. It should not leave Analyze if the causes are only opinions. It should not leave Improve if the countermeasures have not been tested. It should not leave Control if the process is not stable and the ownership is unclear.

The purpose of DMAIC is not to create a project binder. The purpose is to improve a business condition using disciplined problem solving.

## Matching the Method to the Problem

Not every problem requires the same method.

Some problems are simple abnormalities that require immediate correction and local follow-up. Some are recurring issues that require root cause analysis. Some are cross-functional problems that require an A3. Some are complex performance gaps that require DMAIC. Some are system-level problems that require value stream analysis, leadership decisions, and changes to management cadence.

The organization should match the method to the problem.

If every issue requires a full A3 or DMAIC project, people may avoid problem solving because the process feels too heavy. If every issue is treated informally, the organization may fail to address important recurring problems. The discipline is in selecting the right level of structure.

A practical sorting approach might look like this:

- Immediate abnormality: contain, correct, and document if needed.
- Repeated local problem: use simple root cause analysis and countermeasures.
- Cross-functional problem: use A3 thinking with leadership support.
- Complex measurable performance gap: use DMAIC or a structured project method.
- System-level flow problem: use value stream thinking and leadership cadence.

The exact categories may vary, but the principle is important. The method should support problem solving, not make problem solving unnecessarily difficult.

## Leadership Behavior in Problem Solving

Leadership behavior determines whether problem solving becomes part of the operating system.

If leaders reward quick answers, people will bring quick answers. If leaders accept vague problem statements, people will not learn to define problems clearly. If leaders blame people for surfacing problems, problems will be hidden. If leaders ask for root cause analysis but then push their preferred solution, the discipline will weaken.

Leaders should reinforce the thinking they want to see.

This means asking better questions. It means going to see the current condition. It means distinguishing containment from root cause. It means resisting the temptation to supply the answer too quickly. It means reviewing whether countermeasures worked. It means recognizing people for learning, not only for results.

This does not mean leaders should be passive. They should set expectations, provide direction, remove barriers, and insist on progress. But they should do so in a way that strengthens the problem-solving capability of the organization.

A leader can ask, "What are you going to do about it?" and get an action. A leader can ask, "What have we learned about the cause?" and build capability. Both questions may be needed, but they produce different kinds of thinking.

In many organizations, problem solving improves when leaders change the questions they ask.

## Problem Solving and Daily Management

Problem solving and daily management should reinforce each other. Daily management helps the organization see problems early. Problem solving helps address the causes of those problems. Without problem solving, daily management can become a reporting system that identifies the same problems every day.

For example, a daily management board may show that a team is missing its plan each morning. The first response may be containment: adjust staffing, expedite material, or resequence work. If the same issue occurs repeatedly, the team needs problem solving. It may need to understand whether the cause is material availability, staffing variation, machine downtime, unclear standards, poor scheduling, or quality holds.

Daily management provides the signal. Problem solving provides the learning.

This connection is essential for execution reliability. The organization must not only see the gap. It must learn why the gap exists and what to do about it.

## Making Problems Visible Without Creating Blame

A strong problem-solving culture requires problem visibility.

This is easy to say and difficult to create. In many organizations, people have learned that visible problems create risk. They may be criticized, embarrassed, blamed, or given more work without support. As a result, problems are softened, delayed, or hidden until they become too large to ignore.

Leaders influence this behavior by how they respond to bad news.

If the first response is blame, people will protect themselves. If the first response is curiosity and support, people are more likely to surface problems early. This does not mean leaders ignore accountability. It means they distinguish between accountability for the process and blame for the person.

A useful leadership response is:

*Thank you for making this visible. Let's understand what happened and what support is needed.*

That type of response encourages transparency. It also reinforces that problem solving is part of the work, not an admission of failure.

Problems that remain hidden cannot be solved. A problem-solving discipline begins with the willingness to see the current condition honestly.

## Building Problem-Solving Capability

Problem-solving capability is built through repeated practice.

A single course, workshop, or template will not be enough. People need opportunities to define real problems, investigate causes, test countermeasures, receive coaching, and learn from results. Leaders need to reinforce the method through the questions they ask and the routines they use.

Capability can be built at several levels:

- Frontline employees can be taught to identify abnormalities and participate in simple problem solving.
- Supervisors can be taught to coach daily problem solving and escalate barriers.
- Managers can be taught to lead A3s and cross-functional problem solving.
- Project leaders can be taught to use DMAIC or other structured methods for larger problems.
- Executives can be taught to ask better questions, remove barriers, and connect problem solving to business priorities.

Each level has a role. The goal is not for everyone to become an expert in every method. The goal is for the organization to solve problems at the right level with the right amount of structure.

This is how problem solving becomes part of the operating system rather than a specialist activity.

## Execution Reliability Check: Problem-Solving Discipline

Leaders can evaluate the quality of problem solving by asking several questions:

1. Is the problem stated as a measurable gap between current condition and target condition?
2. Do we understand where and when the problem occurs?
3. Have we observed the current condition directly?
4. Are we separating facts from assumptions?
5. Are we distinguishing containment from recurrence prevention?
6. Do the identified causes explain the problem?
7. Do the countermeasures address the causes?
8. Have we checked whether the countermeasures worked?
9. Have we standardized the improvement if it worked?
10. What did we learn that can be applied elsewhere?

These questions are simple, but they create discipline. They help leaders focus on the quality of thinking, not only the completion of an action.

Chapter 5 builds on this point by examining capability. A problem-solving form can organize thinking, but people still need practice, coaching, and reinforcement to use the thinking well in real operating conditions.

# Chapter 5: Training Does Not Create Capability Unless the Work Changes

Organizations typically invest in training with the right intent.

They want people to understand process improvement methods. They want to build internal capability rather than depend entirely on outside support. They want managers, supervisors, engineers, project leaders, and frontline employees to think differently about the work.

These are good objectives.

Training can create awareness. It can introduce language, concepts, tools, and methods. It can help people see waste, understand variation, define problems, use data, and approach improvement in a more disciplined way.

However, training by itself does not create capability.

Capability is created when people use the learning in the work. It develops through application, practice, coaching, feedback, repetition, and reinforcement. A person may understand a concept in a classroom and still struggle to apply it to a real business problem. A team may complete a course and still return to an operating environment that does not support the new behavior.

This is one of the most common reasons training fails to produce the results leaders expected. The organization assumes that knowledge transfer is the same as capability transfer. It is not.

Knowledge means people have been exposed to the idea. Capability means they can use the idea effectively in a real situation.

That distinction is important because most organizations do not need training for its own sake. They need better performance, stronger problem solving, more reliable execution, or greater internal ability to improve the work.

Training can introduce concepts, methods, and language. Capability develops when people apply what they learned to real work, receive coaching and feedback, repeat the behavior, and operate in a management system that reinforces the new discipline. Training should therefore be designed as part of a capability-building system, not as a stand-alone event.

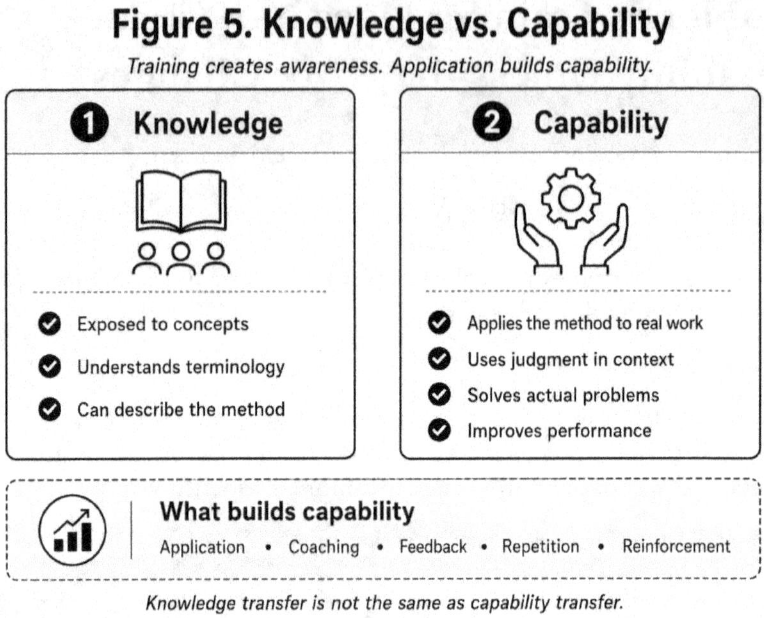


### Leadership Application

*Use Figure 5 when evaluating training requests or certification programs. If the design stops at exposure, terminology, or completion, leaders should not expect sustained performance change. Capability appears when people apply the method in real work and the management system reinforces the behavior after the class ends.*

## Where This Chapter Fits in the Execution Reliability Model

This chapter addresses the capability-building element of the Execution Reliability Model. Training can introduce concepts and methods, but capability is built when people use those methods in the work with coaching, feedback, repetition, and leadership reinforcement.

This distinction is important for leaders because many organizations measure training completion while assuming capability has been created. Completion is useful administratively, but application is what changes performance.

Capability also depends on leadership ownership. Chapter 6 will focus on the management system leaders must own so that improvement work, training, and problem solving are reinforced in the way the business is managed.

## The Limits of Training Alone

Training is often evaluated by completion. How many people attended? How many finished the e-learning? How many passed the exam? How many Green Belts, Black Belts, Lean Practitioners, or internal facilitators were certified?

Those measures may be useful administratively, but they do not prove that capability was created. They show participation and completion, not necessarily application, judgment, or business impact.

In many organizations, people attend training, learn the terminology, complete exercises, and receive certificates. Then they return to the same management system, same priorities, same measures, same resource constraints, and same lack of follow-up. The training may have been well designed, but the work environment has not changed.

When this happens, several patterns are common:

- Participants understand the concepts but do not know where to apply them.
- Projects are selected because they are convenient, not because they matter to the business.
- Managers support the training in principle but do not review project progress.
- Participants struggle between class sessions without coaching.
- Action items depend on people who were not involved in the training.
- Leadership loses interest after the course is completed.
- The organization celebrates certification but does not measure operating impact.

The issue is not that training has no value. The issue is that training was treated as the intervention rather than as one part of a larger capability-building system.

## Capability Requires Application

The best way to build improvement capability is to connect training to real work.

This does not mean every learning exercise must solve a major business problem. People need a safe place to practice. They need examples, simulations, exercises, and guided discussions. But if the learning never moves into the actual operating environment, it remains abstract.

A Green Belt does not become capable by hearing about DMAIC. Capability develops when the Green Belt defines a real problem, gathers data, analyzes causes, tests countermeasures, and learns how to manage resistance and follow-through.

A supervisor does not become capable in daily management by seeing a huddle-board example. Capability develops when the supervisor uses a daily routine to review performance, identify problems, escalate barriers, and coach team members.

A manager does not become capable in value stream thinking by reading about current-state and future-state maps. Capability develops when the manager sees how work actually flows across functions, identifies delays and handoffs, and helps the organization act on what was learned.

This is why project selection is so important in training-based improvement programs. If projects are too small, too vague, too disconnected from business priorities, or too dependent on people outside the participant's influence, the learning becomes frustrating. If projects are meaningful, scoped appropriately, and sponsored by leadership, the training becomes a vehicle for business improvement.

The course should support the work. The work should reinforce the course.

## The Role of Leadership Before Training Begins

Leadership involvement should begin before the training starts.

Too often, training is approved before the organization has clarified what it should help accomplish. Leaders may say they want to "build capability," "create a Lean culture," "develop problem solvers," or "train Green Belts." Those statements may be reasonable, but they are not yet specific enough.

Before training begins, leaders should answer several questions:

1. What business conditions are we trying to improve?
2. What capabilities do we need to build?
3. Who should participate and why?
4. What projects or applications will participants work on?
5. Who will sponsor those projects?
6. How will progress be reviewed?

7. What coaching will be available between training sessions?
8. How will we measure whether the training created value?

These questions help prevent training from becoming a stand-alone activity.

For example, if the business condition is poor on-time delivery, the training should help participants understand flow, constraints, scheduling, material availability, and cross-functional follow-through. If the condition is high defect rates, the training should connect to quality data, process stability, root cause analysis, mistake proofing, and control. If the issue is weak project execution, the training should tie to project selection, charters, milestones, measures, and review cadence.

The training design should follow the business need.

This does not mean leaders need to design every lesson. It means they must define the conditions under which the learning will be used.

## In Practice: From Generic Training to Business-Objective-Driven Application

**Situation**
A biotech organization sent several employees to a generic off-site improvement program. The program itself was not the problem. Participants learned useful concepts and returned with more awareness of Lean and problem-solving methods.

However, the connection to the company's business priorities was weak.

**Typical Response**
The typical response was to view the training as the intervention. Employees attended the course, completed the learning requirements, and returned to their normal work. Managers were generally supportive, but the organization had not clearly defined which operating conditions the training should help improve.

Participants selected projects after the training began. Some projects were convenient or personally interesting, but they were not strongly connected to quality, delivery, productivity, cost, or other business priorities. Other projects required support from people who were not involved in the program.

The training created knowledge, but the business impact was limited.

**What Was Actually Happening**
The issue was not the quality of the training. The issue was that the training was not embedded in a capability-building system.

Projects had not been selected before the training began. Sponsors had not agreed on the business conditions the projects should improve. There was no clear review cadence after each training session. Participants were expected to apply the methods, but the work environment had not been designed to support application.

In that situation, the organization was treating knowledge transfer as capability transfer. Those are not the same.

**What Changed**

The next effort began differently. Leadership first identified the business objectives that mattered most. The discussion was not simply, "Who should be trained?" The better question was, "What business conditions do we need to improve, and what capability do people need in order to improve them?"

The leadership team identified several practical areas of focus: reducing recurring quality issues, improving flow in selected processes, strengthening project follow-through, and developing internal problem solvers who could work on measurable operating gaps.

Participants were selected based on their roles and their ability to influence those conditions. Projects were not treated as assignments added after the course. They were part of the learning design. Each participant was expected to define a real problem, understand the current condition, gather facts, identify causes, develop countermeasures, and show progress against the business objective.

Sponsors were assigned, project reviews were built into the program, and coaching was provided between formal learning sessions.

**Result**

The training became more than a course. It became a practical way to build capability while improving the business.

Participants received feedback while they were applying the method. Some problem statements were clarified. Some measures were improved. Some causes were challenged because they were assumptions rather than facts. Some countermeasures required support from managers or other functions. These issues became part of the learning because they reflected the real difficulty of applying the method.

Leadership also learned from the process. Leaders could see which projects were progressing, where participants needed support, and where the management system itself was creating barriers.

**Execution Reliability Lesson**
Training is most effective when it is connected to leadership-defined objectives, meaningful application, coaching, and review cadence.

The same technical content can produce very different results depending on whether it is delivered as a stand-alone program or embedded in the work the organization needs to improve.

## Client Example: When Capability Revealed the Next Constraint

**Situation**
A growth-oriented organization connected targeted training and coaching directly to active improvement initiatives. The work was not measured only by participation, completion, or certification. Participants were expected to apply the methods to real business issues.

**What Changed**
Training was tied to meaningful project work, leadership sponsorship, and coaching. Participants used the methods to define problems, understand current conditions, identify causes, develop countermeasures, and show measurable progress.

The organization treated the training as part of a capability-building system rather than as a stand-alone learning event.

**Result**
Completed projects generated more than $1 million in incremental profitability. The result demonstrated that capability building can create material business value when it is connected to meaningful work.

The engagement also revealed a second lesson. As teams became more capable, some projects still took longer than expected because decisions were revisited, priorities shifted, and teams waited for clarification.

**Execution Reliability Lesson**
Capability building can create significant value, but capability alone does not guarantee speed of execution. As people become more capable, the next constraint may appear in the leadership decision system.

Training creates value when it is connected to real work. Leadership cadence determines how quickly that value is realized.

## Training Should Create a Common Language

One legitimate purpose of training is to create a common language.

When people use terms differently, improvement work becomes more difficult. One person may define a problem as a solution. Another may define it as a complaint. Another may define it as a metric gap. One team may treat a root cause as the person who made a mistake, while another understands that root cause should be connected to process conditions.

Training helps create shared understanding.

For example, A3 thinking can create a common way to discuss current condition, target condition, causes, countermeasures, results, and next steps. Value stream mapping can create a common way to see flow, waiting, inventory, and handoffs. Daily management can create a common way to review performance, identify abnormalities, escalate barriers, and verify follow-through.

This common language is useful, but it must not become the end goal.

The goal is not for people to use the terminology perfectly. The goal is for people to think and act more effectively. A company can use Lean words and still fail to improve. Another company may use simple language and make excellent progress because the thinking is sound and the follow-through is strong.

The language matters only to the extent that it improves understanding and action.

## Coaching Converts Knowledge into Judgment

Training can explain what to do. Coaching helps people learn how to think through a real situation.

This is why coaching is so important after and between training sessions. Participants often understand the concept in general but struggle when the situation becomes specific.

For example, a participant may know that a problem statement should be measurable, but still write one that is too broad. Another may know that root cause analysis should avoid blame, but still identify "operator error" as the cause. Another may know that countermeasures should address the cause, but still propose a solution that does not match the evidence.

Coaching helps correct these issues while the learning is still fresh.

A good coach does not simply give answers. The coach asks questions that improve thinking:

1. What is the actual gap?
2. How do we know this is the problem?
3. Where did the data come from?
4. What have we observed directly?
5. What assumptions are we making?
6. Does this countermeasure address the cause or only the symptom?
7. How will we know whether the change worked?
8. Who needs to be involved for this to be implemented?

These questions develop judgment. Over time, participants begin to ask themselves the same questions. That is when capability begins to form.

This is also where technology can help when it is designed properly. AI-enabled coaching tools can provide feedback between live coaching sessions, help participants improve problem statements, challenge assumptions, and reinforce the method. They should not replace leadership or expert coaching, but they can make support more available at the point of need.

The important point is that learners need feedback while they are applying the method, not only after the course is finished.

## The Work Environment Must Support the New Behavior

Even strong training and coaching can fail if the work environment does not support the new behavior.

A participant may learn disciplined problem solving, but if the manager wants immediate solutions without understanding causes, the participant will adapt to the manager's expectations. A supervisor may learn daily management, but if leaders do not respond to escalations, the routine will lose credibility. A team may learn standard work, but if standards are ignored whenever volume increases, the learning will not be sustained.

This is why leadership ownership matters.

The management system must reinforce the behaviors the training is trying to build. If the course teaches problem solving, leaders must ask better problem-solving questions. If the course teaches value stream thinking, leaders must be willing to work across functional boundaries. If the course teaches standard work, leaders must verify and improve standards rather than treat them as paperwork. If the course teaches project execution, leaders must review progress and remove barriers.

Training and the management system must send the same message. When they do not, the management system wins.

## Certification Should Reflect Application

Certification can be useful when it represents demonstrated capability. It can provide structure, motivation, recognition, and a clear standard. However, certification loses value when it becomes primarily a completion exercise.

A meaningful certification should include evidence of application. For a Green Belt or Black Belt, this may include a completed project with defined objectives, measures, analysis, countermeasures, results, and a control plan. For a Lean Practitioner or Facilitator, it may include demonstrated ability to apply the method, support teams, and improve real work.

The certification should answer the question: can this person use the method in a way that improves work?

This does not mean every project must produce a dramatic financial result. Some training projects are developmental. Some are selected to build confidence and practice. However, there should still be a connection between the learning and a real process condition.

If certification is based only on attendance, quizzes, or exposure to concepts, it may create a false sense of capability.

The organization should be careful not to confuse the credential with the capability it is supposed to represent.

## Training as Part of a Capability System

Training becomes more powerful when it is designed as part of a capability system.

A capability system includes several elements:

- Clear business conditions that define why the training matters.
- Participants selected based on role, need, and influence.
- Projects or applications connected to real work.
- Leadership sponsorship and review cadence.
- Coaching between training sessions.
- Practical tools and templates that support application.
- Measures that show whether the learning is creating value.
- Follow-up after the formal training ends.

When these elements are present, training has a much greater chance of producing business results. When they are absent, participants may still appreciate the training, but organizational impact will be limited.

This is especially important for hybrid and e-learning programs. Online learning can be useful because it allows people to learn at their own pace and provides consistency across groups. But e-learning still needs application, discussion, coaching, and leadership reinforcement. Otherwise, module completion may become the measure of success instead of improvement in the work.

The question should not be only, "Did people finish the course?"

The better question is, "What changed in the work because people completed the course?"

## What This Means for Leaders

Leaders should view training as an investment in capability, not as an event. That means they have responsibilities before, during, and after the training.

Before training, leaders should clarify why the training matters and what business conditions it should support. During training, they should review progress, encourage application, remove barriers, and make time for participants to work on projects. After training, they should reinforce the methods through daily management, project reviews, coaching, and performance expectations.

This does not require leaders to become expert instructors. It does require them to create the conditions in which the learning can be used.

If leaders are not involved, participants may receive mixed signals. The course may teach one way of thinking, while the management system rewards another. In that case, even good training will have limited impact.

## Execution Reliability Check: Capability Building

If capability building is weak, training may create awareness without changing the organization's ability to improve. Participants may understand the concepts, but the work environment may not support application.

When this element is weak, the organization may see several symptoms:

- Training completion is high, but project impact is limited.
- Participants struggle to apply concepts to real business problems.
- Projects are selected after training begins or are not tied to business priorities.
- Managers support training in principle but do not review application.

- Certification becomes a credential rather than evidence of applied capability.

The leadership question is:

**What must change in the work so that learning becomes capability?**

Training has value when it is connected to application, coaching, project sponsorship, review cadence, and measurable business conditions.

Chapter 6 turns to leadership ownership. If leaders want training to become capability, they must own the operating system that gives people meaningful work, coaching, review, and reinforcement.

# Chapter 6: Leadership Owns the Operating System

Organizations typically begin improvement work with good intentions. They train people, hold workshops, run kaizen events, create value stream maps, develop action plans, and identify opportunities for improvement. In many cases, the tools are sound and the people involved are capable.

Yet the results are often mixed. Some improvements are implemented and sustained. Others work for a while and fade. Some projects never move past the action-plan stage. Some training programs create awareness but little application. Some value stream maps identify important opportunities, but the organization does not provide the resources or follow-up required to make the future state real.

In my experience, this is usually not because the organization selected the wrong tool. More often, leadership has not changed the management system that governs how work is prioritized, reviewed, supported, corrected, and reinforced.

This is why leadership owns the operating system.

By operating system, I do not mean software. I mean the way the organization actually manages the business: how priorities are selected, problems are surfaced, performance is reviewed, resources are allocated, people are coached, standards are reinforced, and follow-up occurs.

The continuous improvement function can facilitate this work. Trainers can build knowledge. Project leaders can manage specific improvement activities. Consultants can provide methods, perspective, and support. But none of these can substitute for leadership ownership. Leaders own the system that produces the results.

This chapter focuses on that leadership responsibility. The next chapter will discuss daily management as the operating cadence. Chapter 8 will discuss follow-through and sustainment. Here, the main issue is ownership: who creates the conditions that allow improvement work to matter?

## Where This Chapter Fits in the Execution Reliability Model

This chapter develops the leadership ownership element of the Execution Reliability Model. Leaders do not need to personally solve every problem, teach every tool, or complete every action. They do, however, own the operating system that determines whether improvement work is prioritized, reviewed, supported, and reinforced.

Leadership ownership connects the first five elements of the model to daily management and follow-through. Business conditions, objectives, system view, problem solving, and capability only become reliable when leaders build routines that make them part of how the business is managed.

The next two chapters explain how that ownership becomes visible. Chapter 7 addresses operating cadence, and Chapter 8 addresses follow-through and sustainment.

## Improvement Cannot Be Delegated Away

One common pattern in organizations that struggle with execution is the attempt to delegate improvement to a function or program.

A senior team decides that improvement is important. The organization creates a Lean office or continuous improvement group. People are trained. Some employees become Green Belts, Black Belts, Lean Practitioners, or internal facilitators. The organization conducts workshops and develops projects. At first, there is energy and progress.

Then the normal pressures of the business return.

Customer issues occur. A major shipment is late. A quality problem requires immediate attention. A new system implementation consumes resources. A reorganization changes reporting relationships. A key sponsor leaves. The CI group is still there, but improvement is no longer central to how the business is managed.

At that point, improvement becomes optional.

People may not say this directly, but the message is clear. If the operating review does not include the improvement work, the improvement work is optional. If leaders do not ask about the projects, the projects are optional. If managers are measured only on short-term output and not on improving the process, improvement is optional. If action items are not reviewed, follow-through is optional.

The continuous improvement function can teach methods, facilitate events, coach teams, and help leaders see opportunities. But it usually does not control the priorities, staffing, capital resources, customer commitments, or functional tradeoffs required to sustain improvement. Influence is not the same as ownership.

This is why improvement often stalls when it is placed off to the side of the business. The organization may use the language of operational excellence, but the actual management system continues to operate in the same way. Improvement is added on top of the business rather than built into the way the business runs.

Eventually, people notice the difference between what is said and what is reinforced. They hear that improvement matters, but they see leaders cancel project reviews. They hear that standards matter, but standards are ignored when volume increases. They hear that problem solving matters, but leaders jump to solutions before facts are gathered. They hear that employees should identify waste, but suggestions sit untouched.

People pay attention to what leaders repeatedly review, support, resource, and reinforce. Leadership ownership is not demonstrated by a kickoff speech. It is demonstrated by management behavior over time.

## The System Produces the Results

One of the most important leadership shifts is accepting that the system produces the results.

This does not mean individuals do not matter. Skill, motivation, judgment, and effort are important. But individual behavior is strongly influenced by the management system around it.

If the system rewards firefighting, people will become good firefighters. If the system rewards hiding bad news, people will hide bad news. If the system rewards local optimization, departments will improve their own numbers even when the value stream suffers. If the system rewards activity instead of outcomes, people will stay busy on work that may not improve the business.

A traditional management culture often looks like this:

- The focus is on short-term financial results.
- Departments optimize their own performance.
- Standards are viewed as limiting flexibility.
- Problems are hidden or softened before they move upward.
- Leaders rely heavily on reports and dashboards.

- When problems occur, the first question is often who caused the problem.
- Experts and specialists are expected to solve problems for everyone else.

An execution-focused culture looks different:

- Leaders connect improvement work to business conditions.
- The organization works to improve flow across the value stream.
- Standards are treated as the baseline for improvement.
- Problems are made visible so they can be solved.
- Leaders go to the work to understand the real condition.
- When problems occur, the first question is why the process allowed the problem to happen.
- People are taught and coached to solve problems at the appropriate level.

This distinction has practical consequences. A leader who manages only by the dashboard is looking at what has already happened. A leader who also goes to the work can see the conditions that are producing those results. A leader who asks who caused the problem may get compliance, but not learning. A leader who asks what in the process allowed the problem to happen creates the possibility of improvement.

The system produces the results. Leadership shapes the system.

## In Practice: When Commitment Did Not Translate into Management Behavior

**Situation**

A mid-market manufacturing organization began a Lean initiative with significant enthusiasm. The company had real opportunities for improvement. There were issues with flow, process stability, inventory, and follow-through. The initial improvement work produced measurable gains, and there was reason to believe the organization could continue making progress.

The concern was not intent. Leaders wanted the effort to succeed. Employees were willing to participate. The methods being used were appropriate. The organization had enough opportunity for the work to produce meaningful results.

**Typical Response**

The typical response was to continue launching improvement activity. The organization scheduled workshops, developed action plans, trained people, and asked the CI resources to support more teams.

This created visible movement. People could point to events, meetings, maps, project lists, and early wins. From the outside, it appeared that the improvement effort was active.

However, the activity was not being consistently translated into management behavior.

**What Was Actually Happening**

Improvement activity was announced before the implementation path was fully defined. Workshops were postponed or canceled because managers were pulled into urgent operating issues. Some actions depended on people who had not been assigned time or resources. Project reviews were inconsistent. Managers supported improvement in principle, but the daily and weekly management routines still emphasized short-term output and firefighting.

The result was an improvement effort that was active but not reliably directed. The organization was moving, but not always in a coordinated direction. Some teams made progress. Other actions drifted. The CI resources continued to support the effort, but they did not control the priorities, staffing, operating reviews, or cross-functional decisions needed to sustain the work.

The problem was not a lack of interest. The problem was the absence of a leadership system strong enough to convert interest into sustained execution.

**What Changed**

The leadership discussion shifted from whether the organization supported improvement to how that support had to show up in the management system.

Several requirements became clear:

- Leadership commitment had to be visible in behavior, not only in words.
- There should not be a long delay between announcing an initiative and beginning meaningful action.
- Improvement work had to be connected to business priorities through a review cadence.
- Resources had to be assigned to the work, not merely requested informally.
- A chain of accountability and support had to exist so improvement did not depend on a few motivated individuals.

The focus changed from launching more improvement activity to creating the leadership routines required to support the work already underway.

**Result**

The organization gained a clearer understanding of why the effort had been losing momentum. The issue was not simply the quality of the tools, the willingness of employees, or the competence of the CI resources. The issue was that leadership ownership had not been translated into operating cadence, resource commitment, and follow-through.

Some improvements continued to produce value, but the broader lesson was that the management system had to change if improvement was going to sustain.

**Execution Reliability Lesson**

Leadership commitment is not proven by a kickoff meeting, a supportive statement, or approval of improvement activity. It is proven by repeated management behavior.

When leaders review the work, assign resources, protect priorities, remove barriers, reinforce standards, and follow through, improvement becomes part of the operating system. When those behaviors are missing, improvement remains dependent on enthusiasm, facilitation, and individual effort.

## The Leader as Teacher and Coach

One of the important differences between a traditional culture and an improvement-oriented culture is the role of the leader. In a traditional culture, the leader is often viewed primarily as the boss. In a Lean or execution-focused culture, the leader is also a teacher and coach.

This does not mean the leader must have all the answers. In fact, effective coaching often begins with better questions.

For example, a leader can ask:

1. What is the problem we are trying to solve?
2. What is the current condition?
3. What is the target condition?
4. How do we know this is the problem?
5. Where did we observe it?
6. What are the possible causes?
7. What countermeasures have we tried?
8. What did we learn?
9. What is the next step?

These questions reinforce a different way of thinking. They slow down the rush to solutions. They move the discussion toward facts. They require people to define the gap, understand the process, and test countermeasures.

In many organizations, employees learn to bring leaders answers rather than thinking. They prepare the slide, summarize the issue, and recommend the action. That may be appropriate in some situations, but it can also separate leaders from the quality of the problem-solving process.

When leaders act as coaches, they are interested in the thinking behind the recommendation. They want to know how the team defined the problem, whether the current condition was observed directly, whether the proposed countermeasure addresses a likely cause, and how the team will know whether the change worked.

This is not micromanagement. Micromanagement tells people what to do. Coaching develops how people think.

The purpose is not to make the leader the bottleneck for every decision. The purpose is to improve the quality of decisions throughout the organization.

## Going to the Work

Reports, metrics, and dashboards are important, but they are not the work. The work happens where value is created, information moves, customers are served, material flows, decisions are made, defects occur, and employees deal with the daily realities of the process.

In Lean terminology, this is often called the gemba, or the real place. The terminology is less important than the principle. Leaders need to understand the real condition of the work they are trying to improve.

A gemba walk is not a ceremonial walk through the operation. It is not management by wandering around. It is not a search for someone to blame. At its best, a gemba walk is a leadership practice for understanding reality.

The purpose is to observe the work, understand the process, ask questions, support people, and connect what leaders think is happening with what is actually happening.

This is important because information becomes filtered as it moves upward. Bad news may be softened. Complexity may be compressed into a few charts. Problems may be described in a way that makes them sound more controlled than they are. By the time the information reaches a senior leader, it may be accurate in a narrow sense but incomplete operationally.

Going to the work helps correct this.

A leader who regularly goes to the work can see whether the daily management system is alive or merely performative. The leader can see whether standards are clear, whether team members understand the goals, whether supervisors are supported, whether problems are visible, and whether the process is stable enough to meet the business requirement.

In one California life-sciences operation, an operations leader demonstrated this very well. When he took responsibility for the operation, he spent time with the frontline teams. In that environment, going to see the work required effort. It meant gowning up and entering a controlled area. It meant asking questions, listening, and observing the conditions employees were dealing with every day.

The employees noticed. More importantly, the leader gained a better understanding of the system he was responsible for improving. He was not relying only on reports or secondhand descriptions. He was seeing the work directly.

That kind of leadership presence cannot be replaced by a dashboard.

## Leader Standard Work

If leaders own the operating system, leadership behavior must become more intentional. This is the purpose of leader standard work.

Some leaders resist the phrase because they think standard work will reduce leadership to a checklist. That is not the intent. Leader standard work is designed to ensure that the most important leadership behaviors actually occur.

Every leader already has routines. The question is whether those routines support the operating system the organization is trying to create.

Leader standard work should be built around the work that must be done to support performance, stability, problem solving, and improvement. It should clarify what leaders at each level need to do daily, weekly, and monthly.

For example:

- Team leaders may focus on confirming that standard work is being followed, responding to abnormalities, maintaining flow, and supporting team members.
- Supervisors may focus on supporting team leaders, reviewing performance, escalating problems, and coaching problem solving.

- Value stream or department managers may focus on flow across the process, removing barriers, reviewing improvement priorities, and supporting supervisors.
- Plant managers, general managers, or senior leaders may focus on verifying that the chain of support is working, reviewing key measures, going to the work, and ensuring that the operating system is stable and improving.

The key point is that leader standard work should create a chain of support and accountability. Each level supports the level closest to the work.

This is where organizations often make a mistake. A CI group creates a leader standard work template and asks leaders to follow it. The template may be technically correct, but if leaders do not understand why it matters or how it supports the business condition, it becomes a compliance exercise.

A better approach is to engage leaders in designing their standard work around the operating system they need to create.

The questions are practical:

1. What business condition are we trying to improve?
2. What must leaders do regularly to support that condition?
3. Where must leaders go to understand performance?
4. What measures must be reviewed?
5. What problems must be escalated?
6. How will leaders coach problem solving?
7. How will leaders verify that standards are being followed?
8. How will leaders detect drift?

When leaders answer these questions, leader standard work becomes more than a checklist. It becomes part of the leadership operating model.

## The Role of the Continuous Improvement Function

Leadership ownership does not reduce the importance of the continuous improvement function. It clarifies its role.

The CI function should help the organization build capability. This may include teaching methods, facilitating improvement work, coaching problem solving, helping leaders design daily management systems, developing internal facilitators, and connecting improvement activity to business priorities.

The CI function is at its best when it helps leaders and teams improve the way they think and work.

It is at its weakest when it becomes the department responsible for improvement while the rest of the organization continues to manage the business the same way it always has.

This can create a difficult position for CI leaders. They may be asked to deliver results, but they do not control the operating system. They may be expected to create engagement, but they cannot force leadership ownership. They may see the underlying issues clearly, but they may not have the authority to change priorities, resources, or accountability.

For this reason, the relationship between leadership and CI must be explicit. Leaders should not simply ask CI to "go improve the process." They should clarify the business condition, provide sponsorship, allocate resources, participate in review cadence, and remove barriers the team cannot remove on its own.

The principle is simple:

CI facilitates and builds capability. Leadership owns the operating system.

## What Leadership Ownership Looks Like

Leadership ownership is easy to claim and harder to demonstrate. It is not demonstrated by approving a training budget, attending a kickoff meeting, or asking for a monthly update. Those actions may help, but they are not sufficient.

Leadership ownership shows up in repeated behavior.

Leaders clarify which business conditions matter most. They select improvement priorities based on customer impact, value, and strategic importance. They assign ownership and resources. They participate in the review cadence. They go to the work. They ask about problems without blaming people for surfacing them. They expect disciplined problem solving before major countermeasures are launched. They protect important improvement work from constant reprioritization. They reinforce standards after implementation. They recognize learning, not only results. They remove barriers that teams cannot remove themselves.

In short, they make improvement part of how the business is managed.

This does not require theatrical leadership. It requires consistency. People in organizations are highly sensitive to what leaders pay attention to. If leaders ask about output every day and improvement once a quarter, the organization learns what matters. If leaders celebrate heroic expediting more than process stability, the organization learns what matters. If leaders ask about problems only after a customer complaint, the organization learns what matters.

Leadership ownership is communicated through attention and follow-up.

## The Cost of Leadership Drift

One reason improvement efforts decline is leadership drift.

A leader who strongly supports improvement leaves the organization. A new leader arrives with different priorities. A company is acquired. A reorganization changes reporting lines. A financial issue shifts attention to short-term cost reduction. The improvement function remains, but the leadership system changes.

When improvement is deeply embedded in the operating system, it can survive leadership changes more effectively. When it depends primarily on one sponsor, one CI leader, or one consultant, it is fragile.

This is why execution reliability requires more than enthusiasm. It requires routines, standards, cadence, capability, and accountability that outlast any single person.

Leader standard work, daily management, gemba walks, tiered huddles, project reviews, standard work audits, and coaching routines all help institutionalize attention. They make the right leadership behaviors more likely and more visible.

The goal is not to make leadership less important. The goal is to make leadership behavior more consistent and less dependent on memory, personality, or temporary enthusiasm.

## Execution Reliability Check: Leadership Ownership

A leader who wants to know whether improvement is truly owned by leadership can begin with a few direct questions:

1. What are the top business conditions we are trying to improve?
2. Can our managers explain how their improvement work connects to those conditions?
3. Do we have a regular cadence for reviewing performance, problems, countermeasures, and follow-through?
4. Do leaders go to the work often enough to understand reality?
5. Are problems made visible early, or are they hidden until they become urgent?
6. Do we ask better questions, or do we jump to solutions?

7. Are standards being followed and improved, or merely documented?
8. Do we know which improvement projects matter most and why?
9. Are we building capability, or relying on a few experts?
10. Do we reinforce improvement when the business is under pressure, or abandon it when things get busy?

The answers to these questions reveal whether improvement is part of the operating system or merely part of the language.

Chapter 7 takes the next step by showing how leadership ownership becomes operating cadence. Daily management is one of the primary ways leaders connect intent, reality, problems, response, and follow-through close to the work.

# Chapter 7: Daily Management Turns Intent into Cadence

Many organizations have some form of daily management. They use huddle boards, tiered meetings, visual displays, dashboards, scorecards, action lists, and metrics reviewed at regular intervals. Supervisors meet with teams. Managers review performance. Leaders ask for updates. The routines may be called daily management, tiered accountability, production control, daily huddles, or operating cadence.

These routines can be useful. However, the existence of a huddle, board, dashboard, or meeting schedule does not mean the organization is managing daily performance effectively.

Sometimes daily management becomes a reporting ritual. People review numbers, explain what happened, and move to the next metric. Red conditions are discussed but not investigated. Problems are mentioned but not assigned. Barriers are known but not escalated. Actions are carried forward but not verified. The meeting occurs, but the system does not improve.

That is daily management theater.

Daily management should do more than create a visible meeting cadence. It should help the organization see performance, identify gaps, assign ownership, escalate barriers, support teams, and verify response close to the work.

## Where This Chapter Fits in the Execution Reliability Model

Chapter 6 discussed why leadership owns the operating system. This chapter addresses the operating cadence that makes leadership ownership practical. Chapter 8 will then discuss the follow-through required to turn that cadence into completed, verified, and sustained improvement.

The central question is simple: how does the organization create a routine that helps leaders and teams see reality, respond to problems, and keep important work moving?

Daily management is one of the main ways leadership intent becomes operating cadence.

## Daily Management as Operating Cadence

Daily management becomes useful when it creates operating cadence. By daily management, I mean the routine process by which leaders and teams review performance, identify gaps, assign countermeasures, escalate barriers, and verify follow-through close to the work.

A cadence is different from a meeting schedule. A meeting schedule tells people when to gather. A cadence defines how the organization will review reality, respond to problems, and keep work moving.

**Figure 6. Meeting Schedule vs. Operating Cadence**

*A cadence is different from a meeting schedule.*

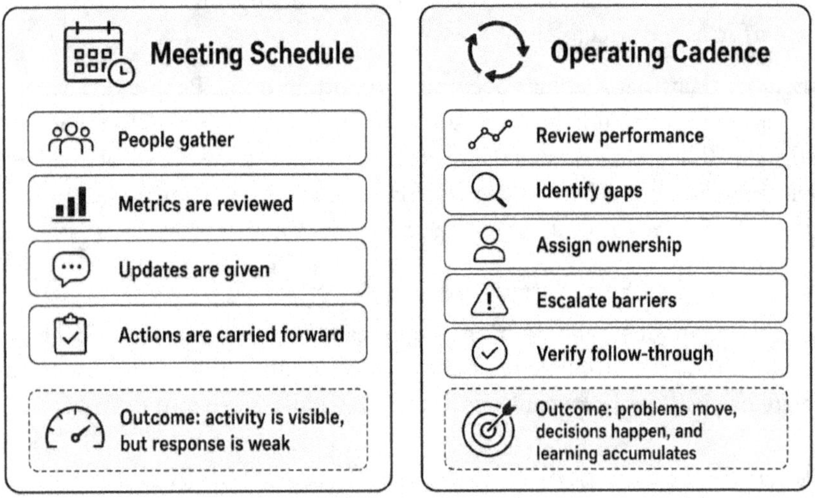


*Daily management turns intent into cadence.*

### Leadership Application

*Use Figure 6 to test whether daily management is producing response or merely producing updates. The right side of the figure should be visible in leadership behavior: gaps are named, owners are clear, barriers are escalated, and follow-through is verified. If the routine stops at reporting, it is a meeting schedule, not an operating cadence.*

Without cadence, execution depends too much on memory, individual initiative, and escalation after problems become urgent. Action items may be captured but not reviewed. Problems may be discussed but not assigned. Leaders may hear about issues only after they have already affected the customer, schedule, or financial result.

In that environment, people often work hard, but the organization does not learn quickly enough. Problems repeat. Priorities shift. Teams wait for decisions. Leaders spend more time reacting than managing the system.

A good daily management cadence reduces this problem. It creates a regular place and time to ask:

1. What was supposed to happen?
2. What actually happened?
3. What is the gap?
4. What is the cause or likely cause?
5. What action is needed now?
6. Who owns the action?
7. When will we check the result?
8. What needs to be escalated?

These questions are simple. The discipline is in asking them consistently and acting on the answers.

## In Practice: When Huddles Became Theater

**Situation**

A San Diego operation had implemented what it called daily management. Each production and shipping/receiving area had a gemba board. Every morning at 8:00, the management team walked from board to board while the area lead reviewed the status of the work.

On the surface, the routine looked disciplined. The boards were visible. The meeting time was consistent. Leaders were present. Area leads were expected to speak to performance. The organization appeared to have a daily management system in place.

**Typical Response**

The typical response was to assume that because the meeting was occurring, daily management was happening. Leaders attended the walk, listened to the updates, asked a few questions, and moved to the next board. The routine continued because it was visible, scheduled, and familiar.

The organization could point to the boards and the daily walk as evidence that it was managing performance close to the work.

**What Was Actually Happening**

The routine was not functioning as a true operating cadence. It was primarily a status-reading exercise.

The area lead read through the board, but the discussion did not consistently identify the most important performance gaps. Problems were mentioned, but they were not always translated into clear ownership, escalation, countermeasures, or follow-up. Barriers that required management support did not reliably move to the level that could resolve them. Recurring issues appeared on the boards, but the routine did not create enough problem solving or improvement.

In other words, the organization had the appearance of daily management, but the system was not managing daily performance in a way that changed the work.

The boards were visible. The walk was occurring. The language was in place. But the cadence was not yet producing response, learning, or follow-through.

**What Changed**
After consulting with an external advisor, the leadership team's focus shifted from whether the boards existed to whether the routine was helping the organization manage the business.

The leadership questions changed:

- What was supposed to happen?
- What actually happened?
- What is the gap?
- Which problems require action?
- Who owns the next step?
- What needs to be escalated?
- What support is required from management?
- When will we check whether the response worked?

The board became less important as a display and more important as a mechanism for surfacing abnormal conditions, assigning response, escalating barriers, and verifying follow-through.

The daily walk also changed in purpose. Management was no longer walking the floor simply to hear status. Leaders were there to understand the condition, support the area, make decisions when needed, and reinforce problem solving.

**Result**
The routine became more useful when it moved from reporting to response. Problems were made clearer. Owners and next steps became more explicit. Issues that required management support were escalated with a specific request. Follow-up became part of the routine rather than something assumed to happen after the meeting.

The organization still used boards and a daily walk, but the meaning of the routine changed. It was no longer just a visible management practice. It became a practical cadence for connecting performance, problems, support, and follow-through.

**Execution Reliability Lesson**
Daily management is not created by boards, meeting times, or management walks alone. Those elements can support the system, but they are not the system.

Daily management becomes operating cadence when the routine helps leaders and teams see gaps, identify problems, assign ownership, escalate barriers, support the work, and verify response. Without those behaviors, even a well-organized daily walk can become theater.

## Client Example: When Throughput Became Visible Enough to Manage

**Situation**
A California public health plan was dealing with a very long claims payment cycle. The organization was growing, the volume of claims was increasing, and the existing process required too much labor and management attention to maintain service levels.

The issue was not simply that people were busy. Claims were taking too long to move through the system, and leaders needed a better way to see the work, understand where delays were occurring, and improve the flow.

**What Was Actually Happening**
The claims process included too many steps, handoffs, delays, and points of rework. Work was moving through the system, but not with enough visibility or control. Leaders could see that turnaround time was unacceptable, but the operating cadence was not yet strong enough to manage the flow at the level required by the business condition.

The process needed to be redesigned, but it also needed to become visible enough to manage.

**What Changed**
The organization examined the flow of claims work, identified unnecessary steps and delays, and redesigned the process to reduce the amount of labor required. Leaders also improved the way the work was managed so that throughput, constraints, and delays could be seen and addressed more directly.

The focus shifted from simply working harder to process claims to improving the system that governed claims flow.

**Result**

The organization reduced the steps and labor involved in claims processing by more than 50 percent. Claims turnaround time improved from approximately six weeks to under two weeks for more than 95 percent of claims.

The improvement mattered because it changed both process performance and management visibility. The organization could process claims faster, with less effort, and with a better understanding of how the work was flowing.

**Execution Reliability Lesson**

Throughput improves when leaders can see and manage the flow of work. In this case, the result was not achieved by asking people to work harder. It was achieved by redesigning the process and improving the management system around it.

Daily management has value when it makes performance, constraints, and response visible enough for leaders and teams to act.

## What Effective Daily Management Requires

Effective daily management does not require a complicated system. It does require several basic elements that work together.

### 1. Clear Performance Expectations

The team must know what should happen. This may include safety expectations, production targets, quality standards, delivery commitments, staffing plans, project milestones, customer response times, or other measures tied to the business condition.

Without a clear expectation, there is no meaningful gap to manage. The meeting becomes a discussion of opinions rather than a review of performance against an agreed standard.

### 2. Visual Performance

Performance should be visible enough for the team to understand the current condition quickly. This does not mean every metric should be displayed. It means the few measures that matter to the work should be clear, current, and understandable.

A useful visual system helps people answer practical questions: Are we on track? Where are we off track? What changed? What requires attention today?

### 3. Problem Visibility

Daily management should make problems visible without blame. If people hide problems, delay raising them, or treat red conditions as personal failure, the system will not work. Leaders need to create an environment in which gaps can be surfaced early enough to be managed.

A red condition is not the problem. The problem is failing to respond to the red condition in a disciplined way.

### 4. Clear Ownership

A problem mentioned without ownership will often remain a problem. A daily management routine should make it clear who owns the next step, what action is expected, and when the result will be checked.

A good board or routine should make it clear:

- which metric or condition is off target,
- what action is being taken,
- who owns the action,
- when the action is due,
- what support is needed,
- how completion and effectiveness will be verified.

### 5. Escalation and Support

Some problems can be addressed at the team level. Others require support from maintenance, engineering, quality, planning, purchasing, finance, human resources, or senior leadership. Daily management should define how those barriers move to the level that can resolve them.

Escalation should not be treated as complaining. It should be treated as a normal part of managing the system. If a team is expected to improve performance but cannot get timely support, the cadence is incomplete.

### 6. Verification of Response

Daily management should not stop when an action is assigned. The routine must also check whether the action was completed and whether it helped close the gap.

This is the connection between Chapter 7 and Chapter 8. Daily management creates the cadence for seeing and responding. Follow-through ensures that the response is completed, verified, and sustained.

## Tiered Daily Management

In many organizations, daily management works best when it is tiered.

Tiered daily management connects different levels of the organization through a sequence of reviews. A frontline team may review performance at the start of the day. Supervisors may then review issues that require department support. Managers may review cross-functional barriers. Senior leaders may review the few issues that require broader decisions, resources, or priority tradeoffs.

The purpose of tiering is not to create more meetings. The purpose is to create a clear path for information, decisions, and support.

When tiered daily management works well, problems do not remain trapped at the level where they were discovered. A material shortage, quality hold, engineering decision, staffing constraint, system issue, or customer priority can move quickly to the level that can act on it.

When tiered daily management is weak, the organization may have several meetings but no reliable path for escalation. Frontline teams raise issues that do not receive response. Managers hear about problems too late. Senior leaders see metrics but not the conditions behind them. The organization has activity, but not enough connection.

The question for leaders is not how many tiers the organization should have. The question is whether problems move to the level that can help, and whether the response moves back to the team that needs it.

## Daily Management and Leader Standard Work

Daily management is reinforced by leader standard work. Chapter 6 described leader standard work as the routine behaviors leaders use to support the operating system. In daily management, those behaviors become visible in how leaders review performance, respond to escalations, ask problem-solving questions, verify follow-through, and support the next level closest to the work.

The purpose is not to script leadership or create another checklist. The purpose is to make the important leadership behaviors repeatable enough that the cadence does not depend on memory, personality, or urgency.

A leader may intend to attend huddles, review red conditions, coach supervisors, go to the work, or follow up on escalations. But if those behaviors are not built into the management routine, they often lose priority when the business becomes busy.

Leader standard work should therefore be designed around the daily management system the organization is trying to create. The practical question is:

What must leaders do daily, weekly, or monthly to make performance, problems, escalation, and follow-through reliable?

## Daily Management Applies Across the Work

Daily management is often associated with manufacturing, but the principle applies wherever work must move reliably from intent to result.

In an engineering environment, the cadence may focus on design milestones, open technical issues, testing status, supplier input, regulatory review, and decisions that could delay launch. In a service environment, it may focus on backlog, response time, customer issues, staffing, rework, and unresolved escalations. In a training-based improvement program, it may focus on project progress, coaching needs, barriers, and application of learning. In advisory work, it may focus on decisions, ownership, implementation steps, and leadership follow-through.

The form will be different, but the management questions are similar:

1. What was expected?
2. What actually happened?
3. Where is the gap?
4. What action is needed?
5. Who owns the next step?
6. What needs to be escalated?
7. When will we check again?

The daily management system should fit the work. A manufacturing cell, product development team, customer service group, project team, or leadership group may each need a different routine. But each routine should help people see performance, respond to problems, and sustain movement.

## Metrics Should Trigger Thinking

Metrics are necessary, but they should not become the center of daily management.

A metric is a signal. It tells the team whether the process is performing as expected. When a metric is off target, the purpose is not simply to explain it. The purpose is to understand what happened, determine whether action is needed, and learn how to improve the system.

This distinction matters because many daily meetings become metric reviews. The group moves from safety to quality to delivery to cost to people, but the discussion stays at the level of reporting. Leaders hear the numbers, but the system does not change.

A better routine uses metrics to trigger thinking. If delivery performance is off target, what orders were late and why? If scrap increased, where did it occur and what changed? If a project milestone slipped, what decision or resource is blocking progress? If a staffing gap affected output, what adjustment is needed today and what larger pattern should be addressed?

The metric should lead the organization back to the condition of the work.

When metrics trigger thinking, daily management supports problem solving. When metrics trigger only explanation, daily management becomes reporting.

## Daily Management and Problem Solving

Daily management is not a substitute for problem solving. It is one of the ways problem-solving is triggered, supported, and reviewed.

Not every issue raised in a daily meeting requires a full A3, DMAIC project, or formal root cause analysis. Some problems require immediate response. Some require containment. Some require simple action. Others require deeper investigation.

The daily management routine should help leaders and teams make that distinction.

If a problem is small, local, and well understood, the team may be able to address it quickly. If a problem is recurring, poorly understood, cross-functional, or tied to an important business condition, it may need a more disciplined problem-solving process.

The danger is treating every issue as either too small to manage or too urgent to understand. Daily management should help the organization respond quickly while also identifying the problems that require deeper learning.

This is where leadership behavior matters. Leaders should avoid using the daily meeting to jump immediately to solutions. They should ask enough questions to understand the gap, the current condition, and the next appropriate step.

## Designing Daily Management Around the Business Condition

Daily management should be designed around the business condition the organization is trying to improve.

If the concern is poor delivery performance, the cadence should make schedule adherence, late orders, constraints, and recovery actions visible. If the concern is recurring quality problems, the cadence should make defects, containment, root cause work, corrective actions, and standard work visible. If the concern is slow project execution, the cadence should make milestones, decisions, barriers, and resource needs visible. If the concern is training application, the cadence should make project progress, coaching, barriers, and business impact visible.

The design questions are straightforward:

1. What condition must improve?
2. What measures show whether the condition is improving?
3. Where should the condition be reviewed?
4. Who should participate?
5. What problems should be escalated?
6. What decisions must be made at each level?
7. How will actions and results be verified?

These questions keep daily management from becoming a generic implementation of boards and meetings. The routine should be designed to help the organization manage the work that matters most.

## Practical Implementation Guidance

Organizations do not need to design a perfect daily management system before beginning. It is usually better to start with one important business condition, define a few meaningful measures, clarify where the condition will be reviewed, identify who needs to participate, and establish a simple way to capture problems, actions, owners, due dates, and escalations. After several weeks, leaders should review whether the routine is helping the organization respond faster, learn more effectively, and follow through more consistently. If it is not, the cadence should be adjusted.

## Execution Reliability Check: Operating Cadence

When operating cadence is weak, the organization may have meetings without movement, metrics without response, visible problems without ownership, and action items without verification.

Leaders can assess the strength of daily management with several questions:

1. Are the daily management routines connected to a specific business condition?
2. Do the measures show whether the work is on track or off track?
3. Are gaps made visible early enough to respond?
4. Does each significant problem have a clear owner and next step?
5. Are barriers escalated to the level that can resolve them?
6. Do leaders respond to escalations in a timely way?
7. Are actions reviewed until completion and checked for effectiveness?
8. Does leader standard work reinforce the cadence?
9. Is the routine helping the organization learn, or only helping it report?

These questions help leaders determine whether daily management is operating cadence or simply a meeting structure.

# Chapter 8: Follow-Through Is the Difference Between Activity and Results

Most organizations are good at starting improvement work. They hold kickoff meetings, conduct workshops, create value stream maps, launch projects, train people, build dashboards, and assign action items. In the beginning, there is usually energy and a sense that progress is being made.

The real test is not whether the organization can start the work. The real test is whether it can follow through long enough for the work to change performance.

This is where many improvement efforts lose momentum.

The organization may identify the right problems. It may select the right tools. It may involve the right people. It may even create a useful implementation plan. But if actions are not completed, if barriers are not escalated, if standards are not reinforced, and if leaders do not verify results, the effort begins to drift.

In many cases, the issue is not lack of intelligence or effort. The issue is that follow-through has not been designed into the operating system.

## Where This Chapter Fits in the Execution Reliability Model

Chapter 7 focused on daily management as the cadence for seeing and responding to current conditions. This chapter focuses on what must happen after problems, opportunities, and actions have been identified. It addresses the final element of the model: follow-through and sustainment.

The central question is simple: how does the organization make sure intended improvement becomes completed, verified, and sustained?

Follow-through is the difference between improvement activity and business results.

## Activity Is Not the Same as Execution

Activity is easy to see. Execution is harder to sustain.

A team can meet every week and still fail to execute. A project can have a detailed plan and still miss its milestones. A value stream map can show the future state, but the future state may never be implemented. A training program can be completed, but participants may not apply the learning in a way that changes the work.

These are all examples of activity without sufficient follow-through.

This distinction matters because activity often creates the appearance of progress. People are busy. Meetings occur. Documents are created. Reports are shared. The organization can point to visible signs that something is happening.

But business results do not come from activity alone. They come from completed actions, changed processes, reinforced standards, better decisions, and sustained behavior.

A simple question can help leaders test the difference:

***What has actually changed in the work?***

If the answer is unclear, the organization may be managing activity rather than execution.

## Why Follow-Through Breaks Down

Follow-through breaks down for several predictable reasons.

1. Ownership is unclear. An action may be discussed, but no one is clearly responsible for completing the next step. In other cases, an owner is assigned, but the owner does not have the authority or resources required to act.
2. Due dates are vague or unrealistic. "As soon as possible" is not a due date. A date selected without considering resource availability may also be ineffective. A due date should create commitment, not simply optimism.
3. Actions are not reviewed consistently. The team may assign tasks during a workshop or meeting, but there is no reliable cadence to check progress. When review does not occur, action items age quietly.
4. Barriers are not escalated. The person assigned to the action may encounter a problem that requires management support. If the barrier is not surfaced or leaders do not respond, the action stalls.
5. Priorities change without explicit tradeoffs. New urgent issues appear. Leaders redirect attention. People are pulled into other work. The original improvement effort remains important in principle, but it is no longer protected in practice.
6. The organization confuses implementation with sustainment. A countermeasure may be installed, a new process may be launched, or a

standard may be written, but no one verifies whether the change is being followed or whether it is producing the expected result.

These problems are common. They do not usually mean people are careless. They mean the management system is not strong enough to sustain the work.

## The Action Plan Is Not the Execution System

Most improvement work produces an action plan.

The plan may include tasks, owners, due dates, status, and comments. That is useful, but it is not the execution system.

**Figure 7. Action Plan vs. Execution System**

*An action plan records work. An execution system gets the work done.*

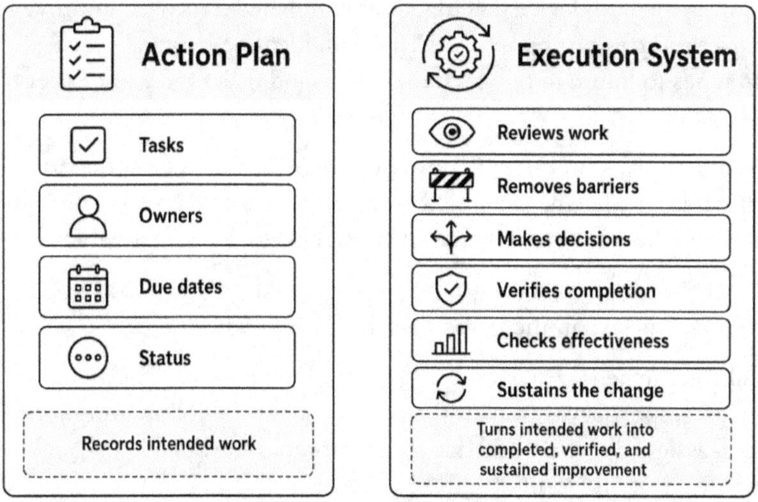


*Follow-through is the difference between activity and results.*

### Leadership Application

*Use Figure 7 during project reviews and post-event follow-up. If the discussion is limited to tasks, owners, and due dates, the organization is still managing the action plan. Execution begins when leaders review barriers, make decisions, verify results, and ensure the new way of working is sustained.*

A project team may create an excellent action plan at the end of a kaizen event. But if leaders do not review it, resources are unavailable, decisions are not made, or priorities shift without discussion, the plan will not produce results.

A value stream team may define the future-state implementation plan. But if the plan requires cross-functional support and no one owns the value stream, the actions may stall between departments.

A training program may produce participant projects. But if managers do not review project progress and remove barriers, participants may struggle to complete the work.

In each case, the action plan is necessary but not sufficient.

The organization needs a follow-through mechanism.

## In Practice: When a Kaizen Action Plan Stalled After the Event

**Situation**
A California medical device manufacturer completed a focused improvement event in a production support area. The team identified several practical opportunities to improve flow, reduce delays, and make the work easier to manage.

The event itself was productive. Employees participated, current conditions were discussed, problems were made visible, some small improvements were implemented during the event, and the team developed a reasonable action plan for follow-up items.

At the end of the event, there was a sense of progress.

**Typical Response**
The typical response was to treat the action plan as the follow-through system. The team assigned owners and due dates, captured the open items, and expected the work to continue after the event.

Some actions moved forward quickly. The visible changes were completed first. The area looked better, and the team could point to several improvements made during or immediately after the event.

However, the more difficult actions began to slow down.

**What Was Actually Happening**
The action plan included items that required support beyond the team's immediate control. One action required a decision from a manager who was not part of the event. Another required quality review before the new process could be used. Another depended on a planning rule that affected more than one department.

Several items remained open because the people assigned to them did not control the resources or decisions needed to complete the work.

The issue was not the quality of the kaizen event. The event identified useful improvement opportunities. The issue was that the event produced an action plan, but the organization had not created a strong enough execution system around that plan.

**What Changed**

The follow-through process was redesigned. The action plan was reviewed on a defined schedule. Each action still had an owner, but the team also identified which actions required leadership support.

Barriers were escalated instead of carried forward quietly. Some actions were rescoped because the original due dates were unrealistic. Actions were not closed simply because a task was completed. They were closed when the team verified that the change was being used and that it was improving the condition.

The action plan became a management tool rather than a list created at the end of the workshop.

**Result**

The work after the event became more disciplined. Leaders could see which actions were complete, which were late, which required support, and which changes needed verification. The team had a clearer way to move from event activity to implemented improvement.

The organization also learned an important lesson about post-event execution. A productive kaizen event could identify the work, but follow-through determined whether the work became a result.

**Execution Reliability Lesson**

An action plan is necessary, but it is not the execution system.

Execution requires ownership, review cadence, barrier escalation, leadership support, verification of completion, and confirmation that the change improved the condition. Without those elements, even a good event can leave behind a list of unfinished actions.

## Client Example: When Follow-Through Reached the Financials

**Situation**

A mid-size medical device manufacturer operating in a regulated environment was facing several connected business conditions: inventory growth, extended lead times, stagnant productivity, and margin pressure.

The organization did not need isolated improvement activity. It needed improvement work tied to operational control and business outcomes.

**What Changed**

Improvement work was connected to the conditions that mattered most to the business. The organization focused on productivity, inventory, lead time, and margin performance rather than treating improvement as a set of disconnected events.

The work required leadership attention, internal capability, operating discipline, and follow-through long enough for the changes to affect performance. Actions were not judged only by whether they were completed. They were judged by whether the business condition changed.

**Result**

Across multiple areas, the organization achieved 50 to 70 percent productivity improvement, 30 to 90 percent inventory reduction, lead-time reductions of up to 90 percent, and a 15 to 20 percent increase in gross profit margins.

The scale of the results mattered because the work reached the financials. Improvement was not only visible in events, action plans, or local process changes. It showed up in operating and business performance.

**Execution Reliability Lesson**

Results of that scale do not come from an action plan alone. They require leadership attention, operating discipline, internal capability, and follow-through long enough for the work to change performance.

Execution reliability should be judged by changed conditions and sustained results, not by the number of improvement activities completed.

## What Effective Follow-Through Requires

Effective follow-through requires more than a list of open items. It requires a routine that turns intention into completed action, learning, and sustainment.

### 1. Clear Ownership

Every important action must have an owner. The owner is responsible for moving the action forward, communicating status, surfacing barriers, and confirming completion.

Ownership does not mean the person must do all of the work alone. It means the person is accountable for making sure the next step occurs.

This distinction is important in cross-functional work. A person may own an action that requires support from other departments. In that case, the owner should be responsible for coordinating the work and escalating barriers, while leaders are responsible for ensuring the needed support is available.

If everyone owns an action, no one owns it.

### 2. Specific Next Steps

Action items should be written as specific next steps, not general intentions.

"Improve communication" is not a strong action item. "Create a daily material shortage review with planning, purchasing, and production by Friday" is better.

"Work on standard work" is vague. "Draft standard work for the order entry review process and test it with two customer orders by next Wednesday" is more useful.

"Follow up with engineering" is incomplete. "Confirm engineering disposition criteria for the three recurring quality holds and update the escalation process by the next review" is clearer.

Specific actions make follow-through easier because people know what must be done.

### 3. Realistic Timing

A due date should be realistic and meaningful. It should reflect the urgency of the problem, the complexity of the action, and the resources available.

A common mistake is to assign aggressive due dates that no one believes. Another mistake is to leave dates open-ended. Both weaken accountability.

The question should be:

When can this action reasonably be completed, and when do we need to review progress?

Some actions require completion by the next day. Others require a short progress check before completion. Larger actions may need milestones. The review cadence should match the nature of the work.

### 4. Visible Status

Follow-through improves when status is visible.

This does not require a complex system. A simple visual board, project tracker, A3, kaizen newspaper, implementation plan, or digital task list may be enough. The point is that the team and leaders can see what is open, what is complete, what is late, and what requires support.

When status is hidden in individual notebooks, emails, or memory, follow-through becomes fragile.

Visibility also helps prevent polite avoidance. If an action is late, the system should make that visible so the team can understand why and respond. The purpose is not to embarrass the owner. The purpose is to keep the work from disappearing.

### 5. Escalation of Barriers

Some actions stall because the owner encounters a barrier beyond their authority. This is normal. The issue is whether the management system responds.

A good follow-through system defines what should be escalated and to whom. For example, a team member may escalate lack of data access to a supervisor. A supervisor may escalate a cross-functional resource issue to a manager. A manager may escalate a policy or investment decision to senior leadership.

Escalation should not be treated as failure. It is part of the system.

If barriers are not escalated, they remain hidden. If barriers are escalated but leaders do not respond, the system loses credibility.

### 6. Verification of Completion and Effectiveness

Completing an action is not the same as solving the problem.

The team should verify both completion and effectiveness. Completion asks whether the action was done. Effectiveness asks whether the action improved the condition.

For example, if the action was to create a new standard work document, completion means the document was created. Effectiveness means the standard is being used and the process is more stable.

If the action was to adjust a scheduling rule, completion means the rule was changed. Effectiveness means schedule adherence, flow, or delivery reliability improved.

If the action was to retrain employees, completion means the training occurred. Effectiveness means the error, variation, or performance gap was reduced.

This is where many organizations stop too soon. They close the action because the task was completed, but they do not check whether the task created the intended result.

## Follow-Through and Standard Work

Standard work is one of the most important mechanisms for sustaining improvement.

When a better method is developed, it should become the new standard when appropriate. This does not mean the process can never change again. It means the organization has defined the current best-known way to perform the work until a better method is developed.

Without standard work, improvement can depend too much on memory and individual preference. A team may improve the process during a workshop, but if the new method is not documented, taught, verified, and reinforced, people may gradually return to the old way.

This is especially common when volume increases, staffing changes, leaders are absent, or a new urgent issue appears. Under pressure, organizations tend to return to familiar routines unless the new method has been built into the operating system.

Standard work helps prevent this regression.

However, standard work is not only a document. It must be supported by training, visual controls, leader standard work, audits, and problem-solving routines. A standard that is written but not followed is not a standard. It is a file.

The question should be:

*How will we make the improved way of working visible, teachable, and sustainable?*

## Audits as Learning Routines

The word audit can create resistance because many people associate audits with policing. That is not the intent in a strong improvement system.

A good audit is a verification and learning routine. It helps the organization determine whether the standard is being followed, whether the standard is effective, and whether conditions have changed.

For example, after a 5S improvement, an audit can help determine whether the workplace is being maintained. After a standard work change, an audit can show whether the work method is being followed. After a daily management implementation, an audit can show whether huddles are occurring, problems are being surfaced, and actions are being followed up.

The purpose is not to catch people doing something wrong. The purpose is to learn whether the system is working.

If the audit finds that the standard is not being followed, leaders should ask why. Is the standard unclear? Is the work method impractical? Were people trained? Are materials available? Did demand change? Is leadership reinforcing the standard?

In this way, audits can support problem solving rather than blame.

## Sustaining Is Designed, Not Hoped For

Sustainment should not be treated as the final step after improvement. It should be designed from the beginning.

When teams develop countermeasures, they should also ask how those countermeasures will be sustained. Who will own the new process? How will people be trained? What standard will be updated? What visual controls are needed? What metrics will be reviewed? What leader standard work will reinforce the change? What audit or verification routine will be used?

If these questions are not asked until the end, sustainment is often weak.

For example, a team may redesign a material replenishment process. To sustain it, the organization may need updated standard work, defined replenishment signals, training for material handlers and operators, supplier or warehouse alignment, metrics for shortages, and a daily review of exceptions.

A team may improve a project review process. To sustain it, the organization may need a standard agenda, decision log, escalation rules, milestone measures, and leadership attendance.

A team may reduce defects by changing the work method. To sustain it, the organization may need visual aids, mistake-proofing, operator training, supervisor checks, and quality feedback.

Sustainment is not automatic. It must be built into the design.

## The Role of Leadership in Follow-Through

Leadership behavior determines whether follow-through becomes part of the culture.

If leaders review action items consistently, people learn that follow-through matters. If leaders remove barriers quickly, people learn that escalation is useful. If leaders verify results, people learn that completion alone is not enough. If leaders reinforce standards, people learn that the new method is expected.

The opposite is also true.

If leaders stop asking about the work, the work loses priority. If leaders allow late actions to be carried forward without discussion, due dates lose meaning. If leaders celebrate the workshop but ignore implementation, people learn that the event matters more than the result. If leaders ask for improvement but do not protect resources, people learn that improvement is secondary.

This is why follow-through is a leadership issue, not only a project management issue.

A project manager can track actions. A CI leader can facilitate reviews. A team leader can update the board. But leaders must create the environment in which follow-through is expected, supported, and reinforced.

Follow-through reflects what the organization truly values.

## When Priorities Change

One of the realities of business is that priorities change.

Customer needs change. New risks appear. Resources become constrained. A major quality issue emerges. A key person leaves. A new opportunity appears. Leaders must respond to these changes.

The issue is not whether priorities ever change. The issue is whether they change explicitly or informally.

Informal priority changes damage follow-through. A leader stops asking about a project. A manager pulls a participant into other work. A resource is redirected without discussion. A due date slips because another issue became urgent. No one formally cancels the improvement effort, but it loses momentum.

This creates confusion and frustration. People may continue to carry action items that no longer have leadership support. Others may stop working on them but never say so. The system becomes unclear.

When priorities change, leaders should make the tradeoff explicit. They should say one of four things:

- This work remains a priority, and we are adjusting resources to protect it.
- This work remains important, but the timing is changing because of a higher priority.
- This work is being paused, and we will revisit it on a specific date.
- This work is being stopped because the business condition has changed.

Clarity is better than drift.

Changing priorities is not the problem. Unmanaged priority changes are the problem.

## Follow-Through Applies Across the Work

The same follow-through discipline applies whether the work began as a training program, an advisory discussion, a value stream effort, or a leadership initiative.

In training-based improvement, participants may leave a Green Belt, Black Belt, Lean Practitioner, or Lean Facilitator program with useful knowledge and meaningful projects. But if managers do not review project progress, provide coaching, remove barriers, and connect the work to business priorities, the training may produce activity without business impact.

In advisory work, the pattern is similar. A diagnostic conversation may help leaders see value leaks, decision gaps, capability issues, or weak cadence more clearly. That insight creates value only when decisions are made, actions are owned, barriers are escalated, and progress is reviewed.

The form of the work may differ. The requirement is the same. Follow-through must be built into the way the organization manages the work after the initial event, class, review, or recommendation.

Insight is useful. Follow-through creates value.

## Detecting Drift Early

A strong follow-through system helps leaders detect drift early.

Drift is the gradual movement away from the intended direction. It is usually not dramatic at first. One action is late. One review is skipped. One standard is not followed. One escalation is ignored. One project is delayed because someone is pulled into another priority.

Individually, each issue may seem small. Together, they signal that the operating system is weakening.

Leaders should look for early signs of drift:

- Action items repeatedly carried forward without progress.
- Due dates changed without explanation.
- Review meetings canceled or shortened.
- Metrics reviewed without discussion of gaps.

- Problems resurfacing after countermeasures were supposedly implemented.
- Standards not being followed under pressure.
- Escalations not receiving timely response.
- Teams uncertain about whether the work still matters.

When these signs appear, leaders should not wait until the initiative fails. They should intervene early to clarify priorities, remove barriers, adjust scope, or reinforce the cadence.

Drift is easier to correct early than late.

## Execution Reliability Check: Follow-Through and Sustainment

If follow-through is weak, improvement work may start well but fail to change the business condition. Action plans may exist, but the organization does not consistently complete actions, remove barriers, verify results, or standardize the new way of working.

Leaders can assess the strength of follow-through with several questions:

1. Does every important action have a clear owner and specific next step?
2. Are due dates realistic, visible, and reviewed on a defined cadence?
3. Are barriers escalated to the level that can resolve them?
4. Do leaders respond to escalations in a timely way?
5. Are completed actions checked for effectiveness, not just completion?
6. Are successful changes built into standard work?
7. Are audits or verification routines used to sustain the change?
8. Are priority changes made explicitly rather than through drift?
9. Can leaders point to what has actually changed in the work?

These questions help leaders determine whether the organization has an execution system or only an action list.

# Chapter 9: The Outside View

## Helping Leaders See the System They Are Inside

Most leaders do not need another initiative.

They already have strategic plans, operating reviews, improvement projects, dashboards, training programs, internal continuous improvement resources, and functional leaders working hard to improve performance. The organization is often not short on effort or ideas.

The problem is that the organization may still struggle to see the operating system clearly.

Leaders are close to the work, but they are also inside the system they are trying to improve. They live with the priorities, constraints, assumptions, metrics, history, and tradeoffs of the business every day. That closeness gives them context. It can also make some patterns difficult to see.

Expedites can begin to look normal. Long lead times can become accepted. Repeated decision delays can become part of the culture. Cross-functional friction can be treated as the cost of doing business. Workarounds can become invisible because everyone knows how to navigate them.

This is where a structured outside perspective can be valuable.

By outside perspective, I do not mean a generic opinion from someone unfamiliar with the business. I mean a practical operating perspective that helps leaders examine the business condition, value at stake, decision path, execution risks, leadership cadence, and follow-through required to make progress reliable.

This perspective does not replace leadership ownership. That would be the wrong model. Leaders still own the business, the decisions, the resources, and the operating system. The value is that it helps leaders see, decide, and act more clearly.

## Where This Chapter Fits in the Execution Reliability Model

The earlier chapters described the operating conditions required for reliable execution: business condition clarity, agreement on objectives and value, system view, problem-solving discipline, capability building, leadership ownership, cadence, and follow-through.

This chapter adds a supporting mechanism: structured outside perspective. It is not one of the core elements of the model in the same way that leadership ownership, cadence, or follow-through are core elements. Rather, it helps leaders work on those elements when they are too close to the system to see where execution is breaking down.

This perspective is most useful when leaders need to challenge assumptions, identify value leaks, pressure-test priorities, improve decision quality, reduce implementation risk, or strengthen follow-through. It helps leadership teams examine the system they are operating inside.

The purpose is not to add advisory support for its own sake. The purpose is to improve execution reliability by helping leaders see the conditions that determine whether improvement work becomes business performance.

## Why Internal Perspective Is Not Always Enough

Internal leaders understand the business in ways an outsider never will. They know the history, the people, the customers, the technology, the constraints, the culture, and the market pressures. That knowledge is essential. No outside perspective should be treated as a substitute for it.

However, internal perspective has limits. These limits are not personal weaknesses. They are normal consequences of working inside a system every day.

The first limitation is familiarity. When people live with a process long enough, abnormal conditions can begin to look normal. The organization may have lived with late engineering releases, excessive handoffs, poor material visibility, unclear decision rights, or repeated customer expedites for so long that they are no longer treated as operating problems. They are simply part of how work gets done.

The second limitation is role pressure. Internal leaders have to manage relationships, protect their functions, meet short-term goals, and navigate tradeoffs. A leader may see a problem but hesitate to name it directly because doing so could create conflict, expose a sensitive decision, or force a resource tradeoff the organization has been avoiding.

The third limitation is fragmentation. Each function sees part of the system. Operations may see production constraints. Engineering may see design or release issues. Quality may see compliance and defect patterns. Finance may see cost and margin. Sales may see customer pressure. Each view may be valid, but the organization can still lack a shared understanding of the end-to-end system.

The fourth limitation is bandwidth. Leaders may know what needs attention, but urgent issues consume the calendar. The organization continues to operate. Meetings are held. Metrics are reviewed. Problems are escalated. But the deeper system questions remain unresolved.

A practical external perspective can help by creating the space and structure to examine those questions. The value is not that the outside person knows more about the business than the leadership team. The value is that a structured perspective can help leaders see patterns, ask different questions, and focus attention on the conditions that determine execution.

## Outside Perspective Is a Leadership Mechanism, Not a Substitute

Outside perspective should strengthen leadership ownership, not weaken it.

This distinction matters. A poor advisory model can create dependency. Leaders wait for the consultant to diagnose, decide, facilitate, or drive the work. The outside person becomes the energy source. When that person leaves, the work slows. That is not execution reliability. It is temporary external momentum.

A stronger model helps leaders improve their own operating system. It helps them clarify the business condition, define measures, understand value, make tradeoffs, create cadence, and follow through. The outside perspective may challenge assumptions, provide methods, facilitate discussion, or coach leaders on better questions. But leaders must own the result.

The boundary should be clear. Outside perspective can help leaders see the system, define the problem, design cadence, identify risks, improve decision quality, and support follow-through. But it cannot manage the business for the leadership team.

If leaders use advisory support as a substitute for making difficult decisions, the work will not create lasting value. If they ask the outside person to carry responsibility that belongs to leadership, the organization may see temporary progress but not sustained change. If the work does not build internal capability and management discipline, it has not strengthened execution reliability.

The goal is to leave the leadership system stronger than it was before the work began.

## In Practice: Reframing the Requested Solution

**Situation**
A manufacturing organization asked for help with a specific improvement

method. The request was reasonable. The company had visible operating issues, and the method being requested could help the organization see the work more clearly, identify waste, and develop practical improvement actions.

At first glance, the appropriate response appeared straightforward: scope the work, schedule the session, involve the right people, and provide the requested support.

**Initial Request**

The initial request was focused on the method. Leaders wanted help conducting the improvement activity because they believed it would address the visible operating problem.

That request should not have been dismissed. In many cases, the leader asking for a tool, workshop, assessment, or facilitation support is responding to a real concern. The issue is not whether the request is legitimate. The issue is whether the requested method is sufficient to address the condition that caused the request to surface.

**What Was Actually Happening**

As the discussion developed, it became clear that the organization was not struggling only because it lacked one more workshop or one more tool.

Priorities were not clear enough. Some cross-functional decisions were taking too long. Several improvement actions were not being followed through to completion. Leaders were seeing symptoms in the operation, but the deeper issue was the execution system around the work.

The requested method still had value, but it was only part of the issue. If the organization moved directly into the workshop without clarifying ownership, decisions, cadence, and follow-through, the activity might create useful insight without producing sustained movement.

**What Changed**

The conversation shifted from the requested solution to the operating condition.

The questions changed from, "Should we conduct this workshop?" to a more useful set of leadership questions:

- What business condition are we trying to improve?
- Which decisions are slowing progress?
- Who owns the cross-functional result?
- What value is being lost because the work is drifting?
- What cadence will leaders use to review progress and remove barriers?

- What support will be required after the workshop or improvement activity?

This changed the nature of the next step. Rather than beginning with a broad improvement event, the organization started with a shorter leadership discussion to clarify the objective, identify the highest-value constraint, and determine what support would be required to convert activity into execution.

**Result**
The outside perspective did not reject the original request. It reframed it.

The requested method still had a place, but it was now connected to the business condition, ownership, decisions, cadence, and follow-through required to make the work useful. Leaders gained a clearer view of what had to happen before, during, and after the improvement activity for the work to produce value.

The next step became more practical because it was no longer only a method decision. It was an execution design decision.

**Execution Reliability Lesson**
A requested solution is often a useful starting point, but it should not automatically become the intervention.

Structured outside perspective helps leaders respect the concern behind the request while examining the operating condition that produced it. The value is not in challenging the request for its own sake. The value is in helping leaders connect the method to the business condition, decision path, ownership, cadence, and follow-through required for execution reliability.

## Seeing Value Leaks

One useful role of an external operating perspective is to help leaders identify value leaks.

A value leak is a condition that quietly drains performance, capacity, cash, time, attention, or customer confidence. It may not appear as a single large failure. It may show up as repeated small losses that accumulate over time.

Examples include repeated expediting, excess inventory, missed handoffs, unclear decision rights, projects waiting for approval, engineering rework, supplier instability, recurring quality issues, training that does not transfer, and leaders spending time on issues the system should be able to manage more routinely.

These value leaks are often known inside the organization, but they are not always named as strategic problems. People may treat them as normal friction. The organization absorbs the cost through overtime, meetings, rework, inventory, management attention, and slower response.

A practical external perspective can help leaders connect these leaks to business value. Lead time is not only an operational metric. It may affect revenue, inventory, cash, capacity, customer responsiveness, and management attention. Decision delays are not only administrative annoyances. They may affect project timing, customer commitments, and employee confidence. Rework is not only a quality problem. It may consume engineering capacity, production time, inspection resources, and customer trust.

When value leaks are made visible, leaders can decide whether they are worth addressing. That decision is important. Not every issue deserves the same level of attention. But leaders should understand the value being lost before they accept the condition as normal.

## Pressure-Testing Priorities

Another useful role is pressure-testing priorities.

Many organizations have too many priorities. Each one may be legitimate. The problem is not that leaders are choosing bad things. The problem is that too many good things compete for the same resources, attention, and decision capacity.

When everything is a priority, execution becomes fragile.

Leaders may believe they have aligned the organization because the priorities have been communicated. But alignment is not proven by a slide, a town hall, or an annual plan. Alignment is proven by what gets resourced, reviewed, protected, and completed when daily pressure increases.

A practical operating perspective can help leaders examine whether priorities are truly connected to the business condition and value at stake. The questions are often simple, but the answers require discipline:

1. Which priorities are most connected to the condition we need to improve?
2. Which initiatives are consuming resources but not changing performance?
3. What should be stopped, delayed, or narrowed?
4. Which projects depend on the same people or functions?
5. Which decisions must be made to protect the most important work?

6. Are leaders unintentionally destabilizing execution by revisiting priorities too often?

These questions affect daily work. When priorities are unclear, teams hesitate. When priorities change informally, action plans drift. When too many projects compete for the same resources, leaders spend more time resolving conflicts than improving the system.

Execution often improves when the organization does fewer things with more discipline. Structured challenge can help leaders make those tradeoffs explicit.

## Improving Decision Quality

Execution depends heavily on decision quality.

Many organizations do not lack meetings. They lack decisions that are clear, timely, and durable enough to guide action. A decision may be discussed but not documented. It may be made in one meeting and reopened in another. It may be understood differently by different functions. It may be approved in principle but not resourced in practice.

This creates execution drag.

The issue is not only whether a decision was made. The issue is whether the decision was clear enough to guide behavior. A useful decision should clarify ownership, tradeoffs, timing, resources, communication, and follow-up.

For example, a leadership team may decide to improve delivery performance but not clarify whether production efficiency, inventory reduction, or customer responsiveness is the primary tradeoff. A company may decide to implement ERP but not define process ownership and decision rights. A team may decide to reduce lead time but not agree on which value stream, which metric, or which constraints matter most.

In each case, the organization may have the appearance of agreement without enough operational clarity to execute.

A practical operating perspective can help leaders slow down just enough to make decisions that are more useful for execution. Useful questions include:

1. Who owns the decision?
2. What information is required?
3. What tradeoff is being made?
4. What options were considered?
5. What is the timing?
6. What resources are committed?

7. Who needs to know?
8. How will the decision be reinforced?
9. What would cause the decision to be revisited?

These questions may seem basic, but many execution problems begin with unclear decisions. The organization may not need another analysis. It may need a decision. It may not need another meeting. It may need clearer ownership. It may not need another dashboard. It may need a cadence for responding to what the dashboard already shows.

## Reducing Implementation Risk

Another value of structured outside challenge is reducing implementation risk.

Many organizations underestimate the risks that appear after the plan is approved. They focus on the desired outcome, but not enough on the conditions required to implement it. The plan may look reasonable, but execution depends on ownership, resources, cross-functional cooperation, capability, timing, measures, escalation, and follow-through.

Implementation risk may come from several sources:

- Unclear ownership
- Lack of resources
- Cross-functional resistance
- Weak measures
- Data problems
- Competing priorities
- Unrealistic timing
- Insufficient capability
- Lack of follow-up cadence
- Leadership attention shifting too soon

The purpose of identifying these risks is not to make the organization overly cautious. The purpose is to improve the likelihood that the organization can execute.

If a value stream improvement requires engineering, purchasing, operations, and quality support, leaders should clarify who owns the cross-functional result and how decisions will be made. If a training program depends on participants completing projects, leaders should define project selection, sponsorship, coaching, and review cadence. If an ERP readiness effort depends on process decisions, leaders should clarify governance and decision rights before more development work continues.

The value is not only in knowing what should be done. The value is in increasing the organization's ability to do it.

## Making Outside Perspective Useful

Outside perspective is most useful when the organization has a meaningful business condition but is struggling to determine how to act. This often happens when the problem crosses functions, the value is significant, leadership alignment is incomplete, implementation risk is high, or prior improvement activity has not produced enough movement.

It is also useful when internal continuous improvement resources need executive air cover, when decision rights are unclear, when capability exists but is not being applied effectively, or when the organization needs to reduce drift and improve follow-through.

External perspective is less useful when leaders are unwilling to discuss value or ownership, or expect someone outside the business to carry responsibility that belongs to leadership.

A useful outside perspective should help leaders clarify, focus, decide, and follow through. In practice, this may include:

- clarifying the business condition and value at stake
- helping leaders distinguish symptoms from operating-system issues
- identifying value leaks, decision delays, and execution risks
- pressure-testing priorities and scope
- facilitating leadership alignment discussions
- designing a practical review cadence
- helping leaders determine what should be done internally and where outside support is useful
- coaching leaders and sponsors on the questions they should ask
- reviewing progress and identifying where follow-through is weakening
- helping the organization move from discussion to decision

The test is whether the leadership system becomes stronger. Are leaders clearer on the condition? Are priorities better sequenced? Are decision rights more explicit? Are barriers escalated faster? Are actions completed and verified more consistently?

These measures may be partly qualitative at first, but they should still connect to operating impact. Eventually, the work should help improve lead time, delivery, quality, productivity, project execution, customer responsiveness, or management effectiveness.

The outside perspective does not own the business result. It helps leaders improve the way they manage the result. If the work does not improve clarity, decisions, cadence, or follow-through, it is probably not close enough to the operating system.

## Execution Reliability Check: Outside Operating Perspective

If outside perspective is missing, leaders may remain too close to the system to see recurring patterns, value leaks, decision delays, or implementation risks. Internal knowledge is essential, but familiarity can make some operating problems seem normal.

Leaders can assess the need for outside perspective with several questions:

1. What business condition are we trying to improve?
2. What value is at stake?
3. Where does execution appear to be breaking down?
4. Which problems have become accepted as normal friction?
5. Which functions must work together for the condition to improve?
6. Are decision rights and tradeoffs clear enough to guide action?
7. Are priorities sequenced, or are too many initiatives competing for the same capacity?
8. What risks could prevent implementation after the plan is approved?
9. What cadence will leaders use to review progress and remove barriers?
10. Would an outside operating perspective improve decision quality or reveal risks we are not seeing?

These questions should not become a worksheet exercise. They are meant to help leaders determine whether they are seeing the operating system clearly enough to improve it.

External perspective has value when it strengthens leadership ownership. It has less value when it substitutes for ownership.

# Chapter 10: AI, Coaching, and the Future of Execution Support

Artificial intelligence is changing how people access information, create content, analyze data, summarize issues, and receive support. It is also changing how organizations think about improvement, training, coaching, and execution.

The opportunity is real. But it should begin with the right expectation.

AI will not replace leadership judgment. It will not replace going to the work. It will not decide which business condition matters most. It will not create accountability, remove cross-functional barriers, or sustain improvement when leaders stop paying attention.

AI can help, but it cannot own the operating system.

That distinction matters because organizations often make the same mistake with new technology that they have made with improvement tools: they begin with the tool and assume the result will follow.

The better question is not simply, "How can we use AI?" The better question is, "How can AI help people think better, apply methods more effectively, and follow through on the work that matters?"

## Where This Chapter Fits in the Execution Reliability Model

This chapter extends the Execution Reliability Model into the future of improvement support. The earlier chapters focused on the operating conditions that make improvement reliable: a clear business condition, agreement on objectives and measures, a system view, disciplined problem solving, capability building, leadership ownership, operating cadence, and follow-through.

AI does not replace those conditions. It can support them. It can help people clarify a problem statement, prepare for a project review, organize lessons learned, summarize recurring barriers, or reinforce a method between coaching sessions. But it must be connected to the same operating logic used throughout this book.

If AI is used apart from the business condition, leadership cadence, and follow-through system, it may simply create more output. If it is designed into the operating system with clear purpose and boundaries, it can become a useful layer of application support.

## Knowledge Is Becoming More Abundant

For many years, one of the challenges in continuous improvement was access to knowledge. People needed training, books, consultants, internal experts, and repeated practice to understand improvement tools and methods.

Those sources are still useful. Structured learning and experienced coaching remain important. But access to basic information has changed.

A supervisor can ask an AI tool to explain 5 Whys. A project leader can ask for help drafting a problem statement. A Green Belt can ask for possible data sources. A CI manager can ask for project review questions. A leader can ask for questions to use during a gemba walk. A team can ask for a communication plan, training outline, or summary of lessons learned.

This availability reduces the friction of getting started. It can help people organize their thinking and save time on drafting, summarizing, and preparing.

However, abundant knowledge changes where the real value is. If people can access basic explanations quickly, the value moves to application, judgment, context, coaching, and execution.

This is consistent with the broader theme of this book. The issue is not usually whether the organization has access to tools. The issue is whether the organization can apply those tools to the right business condition, with the right leadership ownership, cadence, and follow-through.

AI increases access to information. It does not automatically create capability.

## From Information to Application

Information is useful, but application is where value is created.

A person may ask AI to define an A3 and still struggle to write a clear problem statement. A team may ask for possible root causes and still fail to distinguish facts from assumptions. A supervisor may ask for a huddle agenda and still lack the leadership behavior required to surface problems without blame. A leader may ask for a project charter template and still not define the business value, measures, or decision path.

This is why AI should be viewed as support for application, not as a replacement for it.

A generic AI response may explain that a problem statement should be specific, measurable, and focused on the gap. That is correct. But a project leader still needs to know whether this particular problem statement is too broad, too solution-oriented, or disconnected from the business condition.

A generic AI response may list possible causes for poor delivery performance. That may be useful. But the team still needs to observe the process, examine data, understand scheduling, material availability, staffing, quality holds, engineering release, and customer demand variation.

The value of AI increases when it is connected to the organization's method, language, examples, expectations, and business context. Otherwise, it may produce content that sounds reasonable but does not improve execution.

## In Practice: AI Improved the A3, but It Could Not Observe the Process

**Situation**
A project leader in a manufacturing organization was preparing an A3 for a recurring process issue. The first version of the problem statement described the frustration, mentioned several possible causes, and included a likely solution.

The draft was understandable, but it was not yet a strong problem statement. The current condition was not specific enough, the gap was not clearly measured, and the proposed solution appeared before the cause had been verified.

**Typical Response**
The typical response was to keep working on the document until it looked complete. The project leader might revise the wording, add more detail, include a few charts, and prepare the A3 for review.

The A3 might look more polished, but the thinking behind it could still be weak. A polished document did not necessarily mean the problem had been clearly defined.

**What Was Actually Happening**
The project leader did not need AI to solve the problem. The project leader needed help improving the structure of the thinking.

The AI-enabled coaching support prompted the project leader to clarify the gap between the current condition and the target condition. It asked what measure showed the problem existed. It challenged wording that was partly solution-oriented. It suggested separating the observed condition from possible causes. It also asked what information had been verified at the process and what assumptions still needed to be tested.

The A3 improved because the project leader was forced to think more clearly.

**What Changed**
The revised problem statement became more specific, more measurable, and

more connected to the business condition. It was also more useful for a sponsor review because the project leader could now explain what was known, what was assumed, and what still needed to be studied.

However, the important work still had to occur at the process. The team still needed to observe the work, talk with the people doing the job, review the data, confirm when and where the problem occurred, and validate possible causes.

AI improved the preparation, but it did not replace direct observation or factual investigation.

**Result**
The A3 became a better coaching and decision-making document. The project leader was better prepared for the sponsor conversation and better able to distinguish between the problem, the symptoms, the assumptions, and the next step in the investigation.

The value was not that AI produced the answer. The value was that AI helped the project leader think more clearly before going back to the process.

**Execution Reliability Lesson**
AI can support problem-solving discipline when it helps people clarify the current condition, define the gap, challenge assumptions, and prepare for better coaching conversations.

But AI cannot see the process for the team. It cannot verify facts, observe informal workarounds, understand the physical condition, or own the judgment required to select and implement countermeasures. It is useful as a support for thinking, not as a substitute for going to the work.

## AI as a Coaching Assistant

One of the most promising uses of AI in continuous improvement is coaching support.

Coaching is often the constraint in training and improvement work. Participants attend a course or workshop, but they need help between sessions. They may be working on problem statements, data collection plans, root cause analysis, countermeasures, implementation plans, or project summaries. The instructor, CI leader, manager, or consultant may not be available every time a question occurs.

AI can help close some of that gap.

For example, an AI-enabled coaching assistant can help a participant improve a problem statement, check whether an objective is measurable, think through possible data sources, identify assumptions, structure a root cause discussion, prepare for a project review, clarify the difference between containment and countermeasure, draft an implementation plan, or identify questions to ask a sponsor or process owner.

This kind of support does not replace the coach. It extends the coaching system.

A live coach brings experience, judgment, organizational understanding, and the ability to read the situation. AI can provide immediate feedback, reminders, prompts, and structure. When the two are used together, participants may receive more support than they would through scheduled coaching alone.

The key is that AI must reinforce the right thinking. If it simply provides answers, it may weaken learning. If it asks better questions and guides people through the method, it can strengthen learning.

## Client Example: When AI Support Accelerated Green Belt Project Results

**Situation**
A biotech organization was developing Green Belt capability through project-based training and coaching. Participants were expected to apply the improvement methods to real business problems, not simply complete the course.

The challenge was that project leaders often needed feedback between formal training sessions and scheduled coaching conversations. They were working on problem statements, current-condition descriptions, data plans, root cause logic, countermeasures, and sponsor updates. Waiting for the next live coaching session could slow progress.

**What Changed**
The organization used CI Navigator as an AI-based coaching assistant to supplement the live coaching process. Participants could use the tool between sessions to receive feedback on their project structure, clarify problem statements, test whether their measures were specific enough, identify assumptions, and prepare for sponsor or coaching reviews.

CI Navigator did not replace the instructor, sponsor, or live coach. It provided more immediate support when participants were doing the work. The live coach still played an important role, especially in helping participants with the final judgment, business context, sponsor alignment, and the last part of the problem-solving effort that required experience and discussion.

In practice, CI Navigator helped with much of the structure and preparation. The live coaching sessions could then focus on the higher-value issues: decision quality, project scope, cause logic, implementation barriers, and leadership support.

**Result**
The Green Belt trainees accelerated project progress and generated savings in the hundreds of thousands of dollars. The quality of the 1:1 coaching conversations improved because participants arrived with better problem-solving structure, clearer project thinking, and more developed questions.

The AI support also reduced the waiting time between coaching interactions. Participants did not need to wait for the next scheduled meeting to improve a draft problem statement, sharpen a measure, or think through the next step in the project.

**Execution Reliability Lesson**
AI-enabled coaching is most useful when it strengthens the capability-building system around real work.

In this case, CI Navigator acted as a supplemental teaching and coaching tool. It provided 24/7 feedback that a live coach could not practically provide, while the live coach remained essential for judgment, context, and the final refinement of the work.

That is the right relationship. AI can extend the coaching system, improve preparation, and help people apply the method more consistently. It should not replace leadership, sponsorship, live coaching, direct observation, or accountability for results.

## What AI Can Do Well

AI can support several types of work in improvement and execution systems.

First, it can help with drafting and organizing. This includes project charters, A3 drafts, meeting summaries, action plans, training outlines, communication notes, and review questions.

Second, it can help with reflection and preparation. A project leader can use AI to prepare for a sponsor review. A supervisor can use AI to think through how to discuss a recurring problem with the team. A CI leader can use AI to prepare coaching questions for a participant.

Third, it can help with pattern recognition when the information is available and appropriately structured. It may summarize recurring themes in project reports, meeting notes, customer feedback, or problem logs.

Fourth, it can reinforce standard methods. It can remind users to define the current condition, clarify the target condition, identify measures, check assumptions, connect countermeasures to causes, and verify results.

Fifth, it can make support more accessible. People who might hesitate to ask a basic question can ask AI privately and get started. That does not replace coaching, but it may reduce delay and increase participation.

These uses are valuable when they reduce administrative burden, improve preparation, and strengthen the quality of thinking.

## What AI Cannot Do

AI also has clear limits. It cannot observe the process unless people provide accurate information from the process. It cannot see informal workarounds, physical constraints, interpersonal dynamics, or tradeoffs that are visible only when leaders and teams go to the work.

AI also cannot own accountability. It can suggest an action plan, summarize barriers, or propose a cadence, but it cannot complete the action, remove the barrier, show up for the huddle, or reinforce the standard.

These limits do not make AI unimportant. They define how it should be used.

## Grounding AI in a Method

AI becomes more useful when it is grounded in a method.

If the organization uses A3 thinking, AI support should reinforce the logic of the A3. If the organization uses DMAIC, AI support should help users think through define, measure, analyze, improve, and control. If the organization uses daily management, AI support should connect to performance gaps, actions, escalation, and follow-through.

Grounding matters because the purpose is not simply to generate output. The purpose is to improve the quality of application.

For example, an AI tool used by training participants should be grounded in the course material, project expectations, sponsor review process, and coaching standards. An AI tool used for daily management should be connected to the organization's problem logs, action review expectations, and escalation routines. An AI tool used for leadership support should help clarify the business condition, value at stake, decision path, and follow-up cadence.

The more the tool is connected to the organization's real operating method, the more useful it becomes.

## AI as an Execution Reinforcement Layer

The strongest strategic use of AI is not as a stand-alone productivity tool. It is as an execution reinforcement layer in the operating system. In that role, AI helps people prepare better, think more clearly, follow the method, and keep commitments visible between formal reviews.

The practical question is where AI can reduce friction in the eight elements of execution reliability without taking ownership away from leaders.

| Execution reliability element | AI reinforcement use case |
|---|---|
| Business condition | Problem statement coaching that helps users separate the current condition, target condition, gap, and value at stake. |
| Objectives, measures, and value | Project review preparation that clarifies expected outcomes, evidence of progress, open decisions, and sponsor questions. |
| Problem-solving discipline | A3 review that tests whether facts, assumptions, causes, countermeasures, and measures are logically connected. |
| Capability building | Training reinforcement that gives participants method reminders, coaching prompts, and draft feedback between formal learning sessions. |
| Operating cadence | Daily management reflection that summarizes recurring issues, unresolved barriers, and questions for the next huddle or tier review. |
| Follow-through and sustainment | Escalation tracking and follow-up discipline that keeps open actions, barriers, decision owners, and verification dates visible. |

Used this way, AI does not become the operating system. It reinforces the routines that already should exist: defining the condition, reviewing the work, surfacing barriers, preparing decisions, and checking whether action actually changed performance.

## Designing AI Into the Operating System

If AI is going to support execution reliability, it should be designed into the operating system intentionally.

Leaders should begin by asking what problem AI is being used to solve. Is the goal to improve coaching access? Strengthen project support? Reduce administrative burden? Improve follow-up? Summarize recurring issues? Support training application? Improve decision preparation?

Each purpose may require a different design.

The organization should also define boundaries. What information may be used? What information should not be entered? Who reviews the outputs? How will accuracy be checked? How will people know when to rely on the tool and when to escalate to a human expert?

These questions matter because AI can create risk if used casually. Poorly framed prompts, incomplete context, confidential information, or overreliance on outputs can create problems.

AI should be governed like any other important tool used in the operating system.

## The Future Role of the CI Professional

As AI becomes more available, the role of the continuous improvement professional will continue to change.

The CI professional will still need to understand methods. Tools still matter. But explaining tools will become less differentiated because basic explanations will be easier to obtain.

The more valuable CI professional will be the one who can help leaders and teams apply methods to meaningful business conditions. This includes selecting the right problems, defining measures, understanding the operating system, coaching problem solving, supporting daily management, helping leaders make tradeoffs, and ensuring follow-through.

In other words, the CI professional must move up the value chain.

The role becomes less about providing templates and more about improving execution. Less about owning every improvement project and more about building capability. Less about running events and more about helping leaders create the conditions in which improvement sticks.

AI can support that shift by reducing administrative burden and increasing access to coaching support. But it also raises the standard. If AI can explain the tool, the CI professional must provide context, judgment, and integration with business results.

That is a positive development for the profession.

## Execution Reliability Check: AI-Enabled Execution Support

Before using AI to support improvement work, leaders can ask several questions:

1. What business or capability problem are we trying to address with AI?
2. Will AI support better thinking, better application, or better follow-through?
3. Is the AI tool grounded in our methods, language, and expectations?
4. What information will users provide, what information should they not provide, and what risks need to be managed?
5. How will users verify the accuracy and usefulness of the output?
6. How will AI support, rather than replace, coaching and leadership review?
7. What human judgment is still required?
8. How will AI-enabled support connect to training, daily management, problem solving, or project execution?
9. How will we know whether AI is improving execution rather than creating more output?

These questions help leaders avoid the mistake of treating AI as a novelty or shortcut. They help position it as part of the execution support system.

# Conclusion: Where to Begin

Improvement work should create better business results.

That statement may seem obvious, but it is easy for organizations to lose sight of it. Improvement activity can become busy, visible, and well supported without changing the condition of the business. People can attend training, complete projects, hold meetings, update boards, create maps, write A3s, and generate action plans while the underlying operating problems remain.

This does not mean the tools are wrong. It does not mean the people involved lack effort or capability. In many cases, the tools are useful and the people are committed.

The issue is that improvement methods do not create sustained results by themselves. They need an operating system around them.

That operating system includes business condition clarity, objectives, measures, value, problem-solving discipline, capability development, leadership ownership, operating cadence, follow-through, and sustainment.

Execution reliability is not created by launching more activity. It is created by building the conditions that allow important work to move from intent to action, from action to learning, and from learning to sustained performance.

## Returning to the Execution Reliability Model

The model is most useful when leaders apply it to one meaningful business condition rather than to the organization in general. The practical sequence is simple:

- Start with the business condition and the value at stake.
- Clarify the objective, measures, ownership, resources, decision path, and review cadence.
- See the system that produces the current result, including handoffs, delays, and decision points.
- Use disciplined problem solving to understand causes before jumping to solutions.
- Build capability through application, coaching, feedback, and reinforcement in the work.
- Make leadership ownership visible through operating cadence and follow-through.

- Use outside perspective and AI-enabled support to strengthen the system, not to replace judgment or accountability.

Leaders do not need to fix everything at once. They need to identify the weakest element for the condition they are trying to improve and strengthen that part of the operating system first.

## Where Execution Reliability Breaks Down

The Execution Reliability Model can be used as a diagnostic. Leaders can look at the symptoms they are seeing and identify which part of the execution system may be weak.

| Symptom | Likely Weak Element | Leadership Question |
|---|---|---|
| Lots of improvement activity, but unclear business impact. | Business condition / value | What condition are we trying to improve, and why does it matter? |
| Projects receive interest but stall before approval or launch. | Startability / decision path | Do we have objective, measure, value, owner, resources, and review cadence? |
| Local improvements do not improve customer or business results. | System view | Are we improving the system or only one part of it? |
| The same problems keep returning. | Problem-solving discipline | Are we identifying causes or only reacting to symptoms? |
| Training is completed, but application is limited. | Capability building | What must change in the work so learning becomes capability? |
| CI owns improvement more than line leaders. | Leadership ownership | Are leaders creating the conditions for improvement to work? |

| Symptom | Likely Weak Element | Leadership Question |
|---|---|---|
| Huddles and boards exist, but problems still drift. | Operating cadence | Does the cadence create response, escalation, and support? |
| Action plans age without results. | Follow-through and sustainment | What system turns intended work into completed, verified change? |
| Leaders are too close to the issue to see the pattern. | Outside operating perspective | Would an outside perspective help clarify value leaks, priorities, or decision quality? |
| AI creates more output, but execution does not improve. | AI-enabled execution support | Is AI improving application and judgment, or only generating content? |

This table is not intended to replace deeper analysis. Its purpose is to help leaders identify where to begin. Most organizations do not need to fix every part of the model at once. They need to identify the weakest element affecting the business condition that matters most.

Once that weak element is visible, the next step becomes more practical.

## Using the Model with Your Leadership Team

The most practical way to use this book is not to launch an enterprise-wide execution reliability program. That would risk creating the very problem this book has warned against: more activity before enough clarity.

Begin with one meaningful business condition. Select a condition that matters to the business now: late delivery, excess inventory, recurring quality problems, slow project execution, weak training application, poor escalation, delayed decisions, or inconsistent follow-through.

Then examine that condition through the Execution Reliability Model. Is the objective clear? Are the measures meaningful? Is the value worth protecting? Does the team understand the system that produces the current result? Are problems being solved with discipline? Do people have the capability to apply the methods? Is leadership ownership visible? Is there an operating cadence? Are actions completed, verified, and sustained?

The value of the model is that it helps leaders locate the weak link in the execution system. The answer is not always another tool, another workshop, another dashboard, or another training class. Sometimes the issue is unclear ownership. Sometimes it is weak cadence. Sometimes it is lack of problem-solving discipline. Sometimes it is failure to verify whether actions changed the work.

Start there. Improve one condition. Strengthen the system around it. Learn from the effort. Then apply the same discipline to the next condition.

## The Final Message

The organizations that improve reliably are not necessarily the ones with the most tools, the most projects, the most dashboards, or the most training activity.

They are the organizations that connect improvement work to business conditions, leadership ownership, operating cadence, problem-solving discipline, capability development, and follow-through.

They understand that tools are useful, but tools do not own results. Projects are useful, but projects do not sustain themselves. Training is useful, but training does not automatically create capability. Technology is useful, but technology does not replace judgment. Advisors can help, but leaders still own the operating system.

Execution reliability is built through disciplined leadership and practical management routines repeated over time.

It is not glamorous work. It is not always dramatic. It involves clarifying priorities, asking better questions, reviewing progress, removing barriers, reinforcing standards, and following up on commitments.

But that is the work that turns improvement activity into business results.

Do not begin with a program.
Do not begin with a tool.
Do not begin with activity.

Begin with the condition the business needs to improve, the value at stake, the system that produces the current result, and the cadence required to make progress reliable. That is where execution reliability begins.

# Resources and Next Steps

If the ideas in this book are relevant to your organization, the next step is not to launch more activity. The next step is to clarify the business condition and examine the execution system around it. EMS Consulting Group has created a companion toolkit to help leaders and teams begin that work.

The toolkit includes the following:

**Business Condition Clarifier** - supports Chapter 1 and helps leaders start with the condition rather than the tool.

**Agreement Before Action Checklist** - supports Chapter 2 and the Startability idea.

**Execution Reliability Diagnostic Worksheet** - supports the full model and can be used in a 45- to 60-minute leadership discussion.

**Leadership Cadence and Follow-Through Planner** - supports Chapters 7 and 8.

**90-Day Execution Reliability Roadmap** - gives readers a practical implementation path for one important business condition.

To access the companion toolkit, visit:

https://emsstrategies.com/execution-reliability-toolkit/

EMS Consulting Group provides practical support for organizations that want to apply these ideas through leadership advisory work, operational assessments, capability-building programs, value stream improvement, project coaching, and operating cadence design.

To learn more, visit https://emsstrategies.com and contact EMS Consulting Group through the website.

# About the Author

Darren Dolcemascolo is the President and co-founder of EMS Consulting Group, Inc., where he helps executive teams improve execution reliability: the ability to turn improvement activity, strategic priorities, and operating intent into sustained business results.

Since co-founding EMS Consulting Group in 2003, Darren has advised and supported organizations in healthcare, biotech, manufacturing, aerospace, electronics, service, and related industries. His work focuses on helping leaders connect improvement efforts to business conditions, measurable value, leadership ownership, operating cadence, capability building, and disciplined follow-through.

Darren brings deep experience in Lean, Six Sigma, structured problem solving, leadership development, and enterprise performance improvement. Rather than treating improvement as a collection of tools or events, his work helps organizations build the leadership discipline, operating systems, and problem-solving capability required to sustain meaningful performance gains over time.

Before co-founding EMS Consulting Group, Darren worked as an engineer, manager, and consultant across several industries. He is the author of Improving the Extended Value Stream and has spoken at national conferences on operational excellence, Lean, outsourcing, and process improvement. He holds a B.S. in Industrial Engineering from Columbia University and an MBA with Graduate Honors from San Diego State University.

# About EMS Consulting Group

EMS Consulting Group, Inc. helps executive and operational leaders improve execution reliability: the ability to turn improvement activity, strategic priorities, and operating intent into measurable, sustained business results.

The firm works with organizations that need better performance across flow, quality, delivery, productivity, project execution, leadership cadence, capability building, and follow-through. EMS helps leaders clarify the business condition, identify the value at stake, strengthen the operating system, and build the discipline required to sustain improvement over time.

EMS brings deep experience in Lean, Six Sigma, structured problem solving, value stream improvement, daily management, capability development, and advisory support. These methods are used as means to a larger end: improving the condition of the business and increasing the organization's ability to execute reliably.

EMS Consulting Group works with organizations in manufacturing, healthcare, biotech, service, aerospace, electronics, and related industries.

For more information, visit https://emsstrategies.com.

www.ingramcontent.com/pod-product-compliance
Lightning Source LLC
LaVergne TN
LVHW022224200926
848481LV00006B/2115

* 9 7 9 8 9 9 6 4 4 2 7 0 6 *